AAT

Qualifications and Credit Framework (QCF)

LEVEL 4 DIPLOMA in ACCOUNTING

(QCF)

QUESTION BANK

Budgeting

2011 Edition

First edition 2010

Second edition July 2011

ISBN 9780 7517 9766 4

(Previous edition 9780 7517 8604 0)

British Library Cataloguing-in-Publication Data
A catalogue record for this book is available from the British
Library

Published by

BPP Learning Media Ltd
BPP House
Aldine Place
London W12 8AA

www.bpp.com/learningmedia

Printed in the United Kingdom

We are grateful to the AAT for permission to reproduce the
sample assessments. The answers to the sample assessments have
been published by the AAT. All other answers have been
prepared by BPP Learning Media Ltd.

CONTENTS

A NOTE ABOUT COPYRIGHT

INTRODUCTION

This is BPP Learning Media's AAT Question Bank for Budgeting. It is part of a suite of ground-breaking resources produced by BPP Learning Media for the AAT's assessments under the qualification and credit framework.

The budgeting assessment is **computer assessed** though some parts are assessed by markers. As well as being available in the traditional paper format, this **Question Bank is available in an online format** where all questions and assessments are presented in a **style which mimics the style of the AAT's assessments**. BPP Learning Media believe that the best way to practise for an online assessment is in an online environment. However, if you are unable to practise in the online environment you will find that all tasks in the paper Question Bank have been written in a style that is as close as possible to the style that you will be presented with in your online assessment.

This Question Bank has been written in conjunction with the BPP Text, and has been carefully designed to enable students to practise all of the learning outcomes and assessment criteria for the units that make up Budgeting. It is fully up to date as at July 2011 and reflects both the AAT's unit guide and the sample assessments provided by the AAT.

This Question Bank contains these key features:

- Tasks corresponding to each chapter of the Text. Some tasks are designed for learning purposes, others are of assessment standard

- The AAT's sample assessments and answers for Budgeting

- Three further practice assessments

The emphasis in all tasks and assessments is on the practical application of the skills acquired.

If you have any comments about this book, please e-mail suedexter@bpp.com or write to Sue Dexter, Publishing Director, BPP Learning Media Ltd, BPP House, Aldine Place, London W12 8AA.

Question bank

Chapter 1

Task 1.1

Select an appropriate budget in which to place each cost listed below.

Cost	Budget
Market research survey	MARKETING
Wages of factory workers	PRODUCTION
Recruitment advertisement for a new finance director in an accountancy magazine	ADMIN
Raw material costs	PRODUCTION
Salary of marketing director	MARKETING

Select from the following budgets:

Administrative overheads budget

Production budget

Marketing budget

Task 1.2

Match the functions listed below to the appropriate department.

Function	Department
Prepares accounting information, pays suppliers and staff, chases customers for payment etc	FINANCE
Recruits, develops and disciplines staff, and ensures that employment law is followed by the business	HR
Buys raw materials for use in the production process	PURCHASING
Makes sales to new and existing customers	SALES
Investigates and responds to customer complaints	AFTER - SALES

Select from the following budgets:

After-sales service team

HR department

Purchasing team

Sales team

Finance department

Task 1.3

A company is hosting a dinner event at a function room to entertain clients and is creating the budget for the cost. Classify each of the costs below in terms of its behaviour as semi-variable, variable, stepped or fixed.

Cost	Behaviour
Room hire	FIXED
Food for attendees	VARIABLE
Hire of waiting staff – 1 required per 20 attendees	STEPPED

Task 1.4

At a production level of 20,000 units a production cost totals £128,000. At a production level of 32,000 units the same cost totals £204,800.

This a variable cost. True or false? Tick the correct box.

True ☑

False ☐

Task 1.5

A business incurs the following expenses:

Heating FLOOR AREA

Rental on storage unit for raw materials AV. INVENTORY

Canteen expenses STAFF

Depreciation of factory building FLOOR

From the list below, select the most appropriate method of apportioning these overheads between two production departments.

Select from:

Number of staff employed

Floor area

Units produced

Average inventory (stock) of raw materials held

....

Task 1.6

The following details are available for four types of cost at three activity levels:

	Cost at 10,000 units	Cost at 20,000 units	Cost at 25,000 units
Cost 1	18,000	18,000	18,000
Cost 2	30,000	60,000	60,000
Cost 3	30,000	60,000	75,000
Cost 4	20,000	30,000	35,000

Complete the table to classify each cost by behaviour (semi-variable, variable, stepped or fixed):

	Cost behaviour
Cost 1	FIXED
Cost 2	STEPPED
Cost 3	VARIABLE
Cost 4	SEMI-VARIABLE

....

Task 1.7

A manufacturing business anticipates that its variable production costs and fixed production costs will be £23,000 and £15,000 respectively at a production level of 10,000 units.

Complete the table to show the budgeted total production cost and the budgeted cost per unit at each of the activity levels.

Activity level (units)	Budgeted total production cost £	Budgeted cost per unit £
8,000	33,400	4.175
12,000	42,600	3.55
15,000	49,500	3.30

....

Task 1.8

Given below are a number of types of cost – classify each one according to its behaviour (semi-variable, variable, stepped or fixed):

	Cost behaviour
Maintenance contract which costs £10,000 annually plus an average of £500 cost per call out	SEMI
Sales car depreciation based upon miles travelled	VAR
Machine consumables cost based on machine hours	VAR
Rent for a building that houses the factory, stores and maintenance departments	FIXED

Task 1.9

Select an appropriate accounting treatment for each of the following costs:

Costs	Accounting treatment
Servicing of office computer equipment	ADMIN
Materials wastage in production process	DIRECT
Depreciation of marketing director's car	MARKET
Bonus for finance director	ADMIN
Sick pay for production workers	PROD.

Select from:

Direct cost

Charge to production in a labour hour overhead rate

Allocate to administrative overheads

Allocate to marketing overheads

Task 1.10

A business produces one product in its factory which has two production departments, cutting and finishing. There is one service department, stores, which spends 80% of its time servicing the cutting department and the remainder servicing the finishing department.

The expected costs of producing 50,000 units in the following quarter are as follows:

Direct materials	£16.00 per unit ← 800,000
Direct labour	3 hours cutting @ £7.50 per hour
	2 hours finishing @ £6.80 per hour
Cutting overheads	£380,000
Finishing overheads	£280,000
Stores overheads	£120,000

It is estimated that in each of the cost centres 60% of the overheads are variable and the remainder are fixed.

Determine the budgeted cost per unit of production under the following costing methods:

(i) Absorption costing – fixed and variable overheads are to be absorbed on a direct labour hour basis

(ii) Marginal costing

Task 1.11

To help decision making during budget preparation, your supervisor has prepared the following estimates of sales revenue and cost behaviour relating to one of your organisation's products for a one-year period.

	60%	100%
Activity level		
Sales and production (thousands of units)	36	60
	£'000	£'000
Sales	432	720
Production costs – variable and fixed	366	510
Sales, distribution and administration costs – variable and fixed	126	150

7

The normal level of activity for the current year is 60,000 units, and fixed costs are incurred evenly throughout the year.

There were no inventories (stocks) of the product at the start of the quarter, in which 16,500 units were made and 13,500 units were sold. Actual fixed costs were the same as budgeted.

You may assume that sales price and variable costs per unit are as budgeted.

(a) **Complete the following using absorption costing:**

	£
Fixed production costs absorbed by the product	
Over/under absorption of fixed product costs	

(b) **Complete the following to find the profit for the quarter using absorption costing**

	£	£
Sales		
Cost of production (no opening inventory (stock))		
Value of inventory (stock) produced		
Less value of closing inventory (stock)		
Total cost of production		
Selling, distribution & admin costs		
Variable		
Fixed		
Total selling, distribution and admin costs		
Over-absorbed/under-absorbed production overhead		
Absorption costing profit		

(c) **Complete the following to find the profit for the quarter using marginal costing:**

	£	£
Sales		
Variable costs of production		
Less value of closing inventory (stock)		
Variable cost of sales		
Variable selling, distribution & admin costs		
Total variable costs		
Contribution		
Fixed costs – production		
– selling, distribution & admin		
Total fixed costs		
Marginal costing profit		

Task 1.12

Drampton plc, a computer retailer, has recently taken over Little Ltd, a small company making personal computers (PCs) and servers. Little appears to make all of its profits from servers. Drampton's finance director tells you that Little's fixed overheads are currently charged to production using standard labour hours and gives you their standard cost of making PCs and servers. These are shown below.

Little Ltd: Standard cost per computer

Model	Server	PC
Annual budgeted volume	5	5,000
Unit standard cost		
	£	£
Material and labour	50,000	500
Fixed overhead	4,000	40
Standard cost per unit	54,000	540

9

The finance director asks for your help and suggests you reclassify the fixed overheads between the two models using activity-based costing. You are given the following information.

- **Budgeted total annual fixed overheads**

	£
Set-up costs	10,000
Rent and power (production area)	120,000
Rent (stores area)	50,000
Salaries of store issue staff	40,000
Total	220,000

Every time Little makes a server, it has to stop making PCs and rearrange the factory layout. The cost of this is shown as set-up costs. If the factory did not make any servers, these costs would be eliminated.

- **Cost drivers**

	Server	PC	Total
Number of set-ups	5	0	5
Number of weeks of production	10	40	50
Floor area of stores (square metres)	400	400	800
Number of issues of inventory (stock)	2,000	8,000	10,000

Prepare a note for Drampton's finance director. In the note, you should use the cost drivers to reallocate Little's budgeted total fixed annual overheads between server and PC production and so complete the following:

	Allocated overheads to Server £	Allocated overheads to PC £
Set-up costs		
Rent & power (production area)		
Rent (stores area)		
Salaries of store issue staff		

Chapter 2

Task 2.1

Explain what a budget is, and how it can help management perform their duties.

∙∙∙

Task 2.2

For each scenario given below, select the option which best describes how the budget is being used in the scenario.

Scenario	Budget use
The managing director reduces the figure in next year's budget for the staff Christmas party by 25%	CON
The sales director divides the costs for client entertainment between his two sales teams, and gives the managers of those teams permission to spend within that level	AUTM
A bonus cost of 2% of sales is included in the sales team's budget for the coming period	MOT
A retail company is wishing to expand its operations and so includes the rental costs of new shops in its budget	PLAN
The purchasing manager informs the production manager there will be a world-wide shortage of material in the coming period. The production manager budgets for a different product mix because of this.	CO-ORD

Select from:

Planning

Control

Co-ordination

Authorisation

Motivation

∙∙∙

Task 2.3

Explain what the difference is between strategic plans and operational plans.

Explain how the management of a business will set the strategic plans and operational plans for the business.

••

Task 2.4

Briefly explain each of the following terms:

Budget manual

Budget committee

Budget holders

Master budget

••

Task 2.5

Explain the procedures that will be followed from the start of the budgeting process through to the completion of the master budget in a participative budgeting system.

••

Task 2.6

You are the accountant at a manufacturing business, where the managing director already thinks the annual budgeting process wastes too much management time. Explain to the managing director why it may be appropriate to use a rolling budget and how this works

••

Task 2.7

You are the new accountant at a manufacturing business. The managing director wants the time spent on preparing the budget to be kept to a minimum. He wants the costs in last year's budget to be adjusted to reflect inflation of costs, and no further work to be done. This is what has been done every year for the last three years.

You discover that some costs included in the budget are always exceeded in practice and so the budget is ignored by some managers.

Write a memo to the managing director explaining why this method of budgeting may be inappropriate, and suggesting an alternative.

••

Chapter 3

Task 3.1

From the list below, suggest where each of the following sources of information might be obtained:

Source

The previous year's financial statements for a competitor company   *COMP. HOUSE*

Previous month's discounts allowed   *INT. ACCOUNTS*

Industry average profit margin   *TRADE ASSOC*

Information about a competitor's success   *FIN. PRESS*

Average sick days of employees per month   *HR DEPT*

Select from

- Financial press
- Companies House
- HR department
- Trade association
- Internal accounting records

Task 3.2

The labour usage budget will require which figures?

Select from

- Forecast labour hours per unit and labour cost per hour
- Forecast production units and labour cost per unit
- Forecast sales units and labour hours per unit
- Forecast production units and labour hours per unit ✓

Task 3.3

If the material cost per kg, and the materials usage budget are already forecast, what other information is required to construct the materials purchases budget?

Select from

- Production budget
- Opening and closing inventory (stock) of finished goods
- Sales budget
- Opening and closing inventory (stock) of raw material ✓

··

Task 3.4

Explain why it is important to produce a capital budget.

··

Task 3.5

Briefly explain what figures would appear in each of the resource budgets that a manufacturing organisation would be likely to prepare and how these figures would be determined.

··

Task 3.6

Forecasting is an important technique for budgeting purposes, however, it has limitations. Explain the general limitations of forecasting.

··

Task 3.7

Analysis of historical sales data shows a growth trend of 3.5% per quarter. The sales in quarter 1 were 122,000 units.

The time series analysis has also indicated the following seasonal variations:

Quarter 1	+6,000 units
Quarter 2 126.270	−8,000 units
Quarter 3 130689	+12,000 units
Quarter 4 135263	−10,000 units

The forecast sales in units for the remaining three quarters are

Quarter 2	
Quarter 3	
Quarter 4	

Task 3.8

The trend figures for sales in units for a business for the four quarters of last year are given below:

Quarter 1	320,000
Quarter 2	325,000
Quarter 3	330,000
Quarter 4	335,000

The seasonal variations are expressed as follows:

Quarter 1	−18%
Quarter 2	+21%
Quarter 3	+7%
Quarter 4	−10%

What are the forecast sales for each of the quarters of next year?

Quarter 1	278.800
Quarter 2	417 450
Quarter 3	374.500
Quarter 4	319 500

Task 3.9

What are the limitations of using time series analysis to forecast figures?

Task 3.10

(a) Explain the five stages of the product life cycle and how costs and income will alter in each of the five stages.

(b) How does knowledge of the product life cycle affect forecasting of future sales?

Task 3.11

At which stage in the product life cycle is time series analysis most likely to produce a fairly accurate figure for future sales?

Select from:

- Development
- Launch ,
- Growth
- Maturity ✓
- Decline

Task 3.12

The production and sales in units for a business for the next six months are as follows:

	Jan	Feb	Mar	Apr	May	June
Production – units	3,600	2,900	3,200	3,100	3,400	4,000
Sales – units	3,500	3,000	3,000	3,200	3,500	3,800

The variable production costs are £10.50 per unit and the variable selling costs are £3.80 per unit.

Complete the following

	Jan	Feb	Mar	Apr	May	Jun
Forecast variable production costs £	37.800	30.450	33600	32550	35.700	42000
Forecast variable selling costs £	13300	11400	11400	12160	13300	14440

Task 3.13

The direct materials cost for Quarter 1 and Quarter 2 of next year have been estimated in terms of current prices as £657,000 and £692,500 respectively. The current price index for these materials is 126.4 and the price index is estimated as 128.4 for Quarter 1 of next year and 131.9 for Quarter 2.

Complete the following:

	Quarter 1	Quarter 2
Forecast direct materials costs £	667 396	722 633

Task 3.14

The production and sales levels for the next three months are estimated as follows:

	Jan	Feb	Mar
Production – units	4,200	4,400	4,500
Sales – units	4,100	4,300	4,650

Variable production costs are currently £25.00 per unit and variable selling costs are £8.00 per unit. The price indices for the production costs and selling costs are currently 135.2 and 140.5 respectively.

The anticipated price indices for production and selling costs for the next three months are given below:

	Jan	Feb	Mar
Production costs index	137.3	139.0	139.6
Selling costs index	141.5	143.0	143.7

Complete the following

	Jan	Feb	Mar
Forecast variable production costs £	106631	113092	116161
Forecast variable selling costs £	33033	35012	38047

224.6   240.3

Task 3.15

Last month, a company's electricity bill was £35,000. The cost of electricity will increase with RPI in the coming month, but a prompt payment discount of 5% has also been negotiated.

35.574

Last month's machinery maintenance costs were £20,000 when the company had to make 4 call-outs to specialist engineers. The engineers predict that two more machines will fail and require a call-out each in the coming month. Due to rising fuel costs, the cost of a call-out will increase by 5% next month.

10,500

Last month's water costs were £62,000 but were unusually high due to a burst pipe (now fixed), which contributed £15,000 to the costs last month. Water prices increase with RPI each month. *So.285*

The RPI for the last month was 224.6 and the RPI for the coming month is predicted to be 240.3.

The forecast total electricity, machinery maintenance and water costs for the coming month are £ .... *96 359* .... ✓

Task 3.16

Last year's rent was £65,000 but will increase next year by 5.5%. *68575*

Last year's insurance premium was £15,700 but will increase next year by 10%. *17270*

Last year's power costs were £84,000 and these normally increase in line with the average RPI each year. *86475*

The average RPI for last year was 166.3 and it is believed that the average RPI for next year will be 171.2.

The forecast fixed costs for next year are £ .... *172 320* ...... ✓ ....

Task 3.17

The costs of a factory maintenance department appear to be partially dependent upon the number of machine hours operated each month. The machine hours and the maintenance department costs for the last six months are given below:

	Machine hours	Maintenance cost £
June	14,200 ✗	285,000 ✗
July	14,800	293,000
August	15,200 ✗	300,000 ✗
September	14,500	290,000
October	15,000	298,000
November	14,700	292,000

The estimated variable cost per machine hour is £ ..*15*....................................

The estimated fixed costs of the maintenance department are £ ....*72,600*........

Task 3.18

The activity levels and related production costs for the last six months were as follows:

	Activity level units	Production cost £
July	63,000	608,000
August	70,000	642,000
September	76,000	699,000
October	73,000	677,000
November	71,000	652,000
December	68,000	623,000

91.000
13.000
£7 VARIABLE
167.000 FIXED

Complete the following, using the hi lo method to determine the fixed element of the production costs and the variable rate.

State which of the two estimates is likely to be the most accurate and why. 74 000 WITHIN RANGE

Forecast units	Production costs £
74,000	685000
90,000	797.000

....

Task 3.19

If the equation of a straight line defines a semi-variable cost what do the figures representing a and b in the equation mean?

Select from:

- a is the fixed element of cost, b is the variable amount per unit/hour ✓
- a is the variable amount per unit/hour, b is the fixed element of cost
- a is the relevant range of the cost, b is the fixed element of cost
- a is the relevant range of the cost, b is the variable amount per unit/hour

....

Task 3.20

The linear regression equation for the production costs of a business is:

$y = 138,000 + 6.4x$

If production is expected to be 105,000 units in the next quarter what are the anticipated production costs?

Select from:

- 33,000
- 5,156
- 810,000 ✓
- 672,000

✓

Task 3.21

The linear regression equation for the power costs of a factory is given as follows:

$y = 80,000 + 0.5x$

where x is the number of machine hours used in a period.

The anticipated machine hours for the next six months are as follows. Complete the following giving the forecasts for the power costs.

	Machine hours	Power costs £
April	380,000	270,000
May	400,000	280,000
June	395,000	277,500
July	405,000	282,500
August	410,000	285,000
September	420,000	290,000

Task 3.22

The linear regression equation for the trend of sales in thousands of units per month based upon time series analysis of the figures for the last two years is:

$y = 3.1 + 0.9x$

The estimated sales trend for each of the first three months of next year is:

	Sales trend (units)
Month 1	25,600
Month 2	26,500 ✓
Month 3	27,400

....

Task 3.23

A time series analysis of sales volumes each quarter for the last three years, 20X1 to 20X3, has identified the trend equation as follows:

$y = 400 + 105x$

where y is the sales volume and x is the time period.

The seasonal variations for each quarter have been calculated as:

Quarter 1	−175
Quarter 2	+225
Quarter 3	+150
Quarter 4	−200

Forecast the sales volume for each quarter of 20X4.

	Sales volume
Quarter 1	1590
Quarter 2	2095
Quarter 3	2125
Quarter 4	1880 ✓

....

Chapter 4

Task 4.1

A business has budgeted sales for the next period of 13,800 units of its product. The inventory (stock) at the start of the period is 2,100 units and this is to be reduced to 1,500 units at the end of the period.

What is the production quantity for the period?

Select from

- 13,800
- 13,200
- 14,400
- 2,100
- 1,500

Task 4.2

A business is preparing its production budget for the next quarter. It is estimated that 200,000 units of the product can be sold in the quarter and the opening inventory is currently 35,000 units. The inventory level is to be reduced by 30% by the end of the quarter.

What is the production budget for the quarter?

Select from

- 189,500
- 175,500
- 210,500
- 191,923

Task 4.3

A business is preparing its production budget for the next quarter. It will have opening inventory of 1,500 units but wants no closing inventory at the end of the quarter. Sales are likely to exceed production by 20%.

What is the production budget for the quarter?

Select from

- 1,500 units
- 1,875 units
- 7,500 units
- 9,000 units

••

Task 4.4

A production process has normal losses of 3% of completed output and production of 16,200 good units is required.

How many units must be produced in total?

Select from

- 16,686
- 16,702
- 486
- 15,714

••

Task 4.5

Complete the following production budget for a product. Closing inventory (stock) is to be 25% of the next period's sales. Sales in period 4 will be 11,200 units.

Units of product

	Period 1	Period 2	Period 3
Opening inventory (stock)	2,700		
Production			
Sales	10,800	11,500	11,000
Closing inventory (stock)			

••

Task 4.6

The production budget for a product X is shown below for the next three months.

Quality control procedures have shown that 4% of completed production are found to be defective and are unsellable.

Complete the following, showing how many units must be manufactured to allow for the defective items.

	Period 1	Period 2	Period 3
Required units	12,000	11,000	12,500
Manufactured units			

Task 4.7

A business requires 25,400 units of production in a period and each unit requires 5 kg of raw materials in the finished product. The production process has a normal loss of 10% of raw materials during the production process.

What is the total amount of the raw material required for the period?

Select from:

- 114,300
- 26,950
- 28,222
- 141,112

Task 4.8

The production budget for the product is 40,000 units in the quarter.

Each unit of product requires 5 kgs of raw material. Opening inventory (stock) of raw material is budgeted to be 30,000 kg and inventory (stock) levels are to be reduced by 20% by the end of the quarter.

The material usage budget for the raw material is ....

The materials purchasing budget for the raw material is ....

Task 4.9

The production budget in units for the next period, period 1, is 32,000, and for period 2 is 35,000.

Each completed unit of the product requires 8 kgs of raw material; however, the production process has a normal loss of 20% of material. Inventory (stock) levels of raw materials are held in order to be sufficient to cover 25% of gross production for the following period. The inventory (stock) of raw material at the start of period 1 is budgeted to be 64,000 kgs.

The price of each kilogram of raw material is £2.50.

Complete the following

	Period 1
Materials usage budget in kg	
Materials purchases budget in kg	
Materials purchases budget in £	

....

Task 4.10

A product requires 18 labour hours for each unit. However 10% of working hours are non-productive.

How many hours must an employee be paid for in order to produce 20 units?

Select from:

▪ 324

▪ 400

▪ 396

▪ 360

....

Task 4.11

A business wishes to produce 120,000 units of its product with a standard labour time of 4 hours per unit. The workforce are currently working at 120% efficiency.

How many hours will it take to produce the units required?

Select from:

▪ 400,000

▪ 384,000

▪ 100,000

▪ 480,000

....

Task 4.12

	Quarter 1	Quarter 2
Budgeted sales	102,000 units	115,000 units

The inventory (stock) of finished goods at the start of quarter 1 is 17,000 units and it is business policy to maintain closing finished goods inventory (stock) levels at one-sixth of the following quarter's budgeted sales.

Each unit is forecast to take 5.5 labour hours, however, it is anticipated that during quarter 1, due to technical problems, the workforce will only be working at 95% efficiency.

You are to produce the production budget and the labour usage budget for quarter 1.

For quarter 1, the production budget is ....

For quarter 1, the labour usage budget is ....

Task 4.13

Using the information given below complete the following budgets for period 1.

	Period 1
Sales budget (£)	
Production budget (units)	
Materials usage budget (kg)	
Materials purchasing budget (kg)	
Labour budget (hours)	
Labour budget (£)	

The sales forecast for period 1 is 3,000 units and for period 2 is 3,400 units.

The selling price will be £40 per unit.

The closing inventory (stock) of finished goods is to be enough to cover 20% of sales demand for the next period.

3% of production is defective and has to be scrapped with no scrap value.

Each unit of production requires 4 kgs of raw material X and the production process has a normal loss of 10% of the materials input into the process.

It is policy to hold enough raw materials inventory (stock) to cover 35% of the following period's production. The inventory (stock) level at the start of period 1 is 4,200 kgs of raw material. The material usage for production in period 2 is budgeted as 16,040 kgs.

The standard time for production of one unit is 2 labour hours, however, due to necessary break times only 80% of the time worked is productive. The labour force are paid at a rate of £8 per hour.

Task 4.14

The data provided by the sales and production departments for two products is as follows:

	Aye	Bee
Budgeted sales (units) quarter 1	1,500	2,400
Budgeted sales (units) quarter 2	1,500	2,400
Budgeted material per unit (kg)	4	7
Budgeted labour hours per unit	10	7
Opening units of finished inventory (stock)	160	300
Closing units of finished inventory (stock) (days' sales next quarter)	5 days	5 days
Failure rate of finished production	2%	2.5%
Finance and other costs of holding a unit in inventory (stock) per quarter	£6.00	£7.00

The failed units are only discovered after completion of the products and they have no resale value.

Other information available is as follows:

Weeks in each quarter	12 weeks
Days per week	5 days
Hours per week	35 hours
Number of employees	70 employees
Budgeted labour rate per hour	£8.00
Overtime premium for hours worked in excess of 35 hours per week	50%
Budgeted cost of material per kg	£10.00
Opening inventory (stock) of raw materials	2,800 kgs
Closing inventory (stock) of raw materials (days' current quarter's production)	6 days
Financing and other costs of keeping 1 kg of raw material in inventory (stock) per quarter	£2.00

Complete the following for quarter 1

- The number of production days are ....
- The closing finished inventory (stock) of Aye and Bee in units is ....
- The labour hours available before overtime has to be paid are ....
- Production budget (units): Aye ....

  Bee ....
- Materials purchases budget (kg) ....
- Materials purchases budget (£) ....
- Labour usage budget (hours) ....
- Labour cost budget (£) ....
- The cost savings arising from the change in inventory (stock) levels for quarter 1 are ....

Task 4.15

The following sales forecasts are for periods of 20 days (four five-day weeks).

Sales forecast

	Sales forecast				
Period number	1	2	3	4	5
Number of Gammas	19,400	21,340	23,280	22,310	22,310

- On completion of production, 3% of units are found to be faulty and have to be scrapped with nil scrap value.
- Opening inventory (stock): period 1
  - Finished inventory (stock) 3,880 units
  - Raw materials 16,500 litres
- Closing inventory (stock) at the end of each period
  - Finished inventory (stock) must equal 4 days' sales volume in the next period.
  - Raw materials must equal 5 days' gross production in the next period.
- Each unit requires three litres of material costing £8 per litre.
- Each unit requires 0.5 hours of labour.
- There are 70 production workers who each work a 40 hour week, for which each employee is paid a guaranteed wage of £240 per week.
- The cost of any overtime is £9 per hour.

Tasks

Prepare the following budgets.

	Period 1	Period 2	Period 3	Period 4
(i) Gross production budget (units)				
(ii) Materials purchases budget (litres)				
(iii) Materials purchases budget (£)				
(iv) Labour budget (hours)				
(v) Labour budget (£)				

Task 4.16

Extracts of the sales and production budgets of a product for the next four quarters are:

	Quarter 1	Quarter 2	Quarter 3	Quarter 4
Production (units)	3,100	3,600	4,100	4,500
Labour usage (hours)	9,300	10,800	12,300	13,500
Sales volume (units)	2,910	3,395	3,880	4,365

Assume there are 12 weeks in a quarter.

The production director is not happy with the production budget because there are only 29 production workers available, paid for a 35 hour week, and overtime is not possible. It is however possible to increase closing inventory (stock), although this should be kept to a minimum.

The sales director is not happy with the sales forecast, and based on data from the past six years, has proposed the use of linear regression to help forecast sales, using the formula:

$$y = 1,000 + 100x$$

where y is the forecast sales trend measured in units of product, 1,000 is a constant and x is the quarter number. The relevant value of x for quarter 1 would be 25.

Seasonal variations.

The sales director has also calculated the following seasonal variations based on the 24 observations:

Seasonal variations				
	Quarter 1	Quarter 2	Quarter 3	Quarter 4
Seasonal variation (units)	(500)	(300)	300	500

Produce a revised labour hours budget and hence production schedule, which removes the need for overtime, and complete the revised sales forecast based on the linear regression equation.

	Quarter 1	Quarter 2	Quarter 3	Quarter 4
Surplus/(shortage) in current labour budget (hours)				
Revised labour (hours)				
Revised production (units)				
Revised sales forecast (units)				

Chapter 5

Task 5.1

A business makes 30% of its monthly sales for cash with the remainder being sold on credit. On average 40% of the total sales are received in the month following the sale and the remainder in the second month after the sale. Budgeted sales figures are estimated to be as follows:

	OCT	NOV	DEC	£
	84.000	75.000	66.000	
August	106.000	112.006	100 000	240,000
September	72 000	79.500	84.000	265,000
October		266.500	250,000	280,000
November	262,000			250,000
December				220,000

Complete the following

	October	November	December
Budgeted cash receipts from sales (£)	262 000	266.500	250,000

....

Task 5.2

A business purchases all of its goods on credit from suppliers. 20% of purchases are offered a discount of 2% for payment in the month of purchase and the business takes advantage of these discounts. A further 45% of purchases are paid for in the month after the purchase and the remainder two months after the purchase. Purchases figures are estimated to be as follows:

	OCT	NOV	DEC	£
August	37.240	39 200	43120	180,000
September	74.250	85 500	90.000	165,000
October	63 000	57 750	66 500	190,000
November				200,000
December	174490	182450	199 620	220,000

Complete the following

	October	November	December
Budgeted cash payments for purchases (£)	174490	182450	199620

....

Task 5.3

A business sells its single product for £50 which produces a gross profit margin of 40%. The product is purchased in the month of sale and is paid for in the month following the purchase.

Estimated sales quantities are as follows.

$\frac{50}{100} \times 60 = £30 \text{ cost}$

	Units
July	5,000 *150 00*
August	5,200 *156.00*
September	5,500 *165.00*
October	5,750 *172,50*

Complete the following

	August	September	October
Cash payments to suppliers (£)	*150,000*	*156.000*	*165.000*

....

Task 5.4

Assume no opening and closing inventory (stock)

Forecast annual sales of £6,000 and a mark up of 33⅓%, means forecast purchases of
4500

Forecast annual purchases of £12,000 and a margin of 20%, means forecast sales of
15000

Forecast annual sales of £16,000 and forecast annual profits of £6,000, mean forecast mark-up of ......*60%*...... and margin of ......*37½%*...

....

Task 5.5

A business makes all of its sales on credit with a 3% settlement discount offered for payment within the month of the sale. 25% of sales take up this settlement discount and 70% of sales are paid in the following month. The remainder are irrecoverable (bad) debts.

Budgeted sales figures are as follows.

APR   *MAY*   *JUN*

				£
March	*145500*	*140650*	*133375*	650,000
April	*455 000*	*420000*	*406 000*	600,000
May				580,000
June				550,000

Complete the following

	April	May	June
Budgeted cash receipts for sales (£)	*600 500*	*560 650*	*539 375*

....

Task 5.6

A business manufactures and sells a single product, each unit of which requires 20 minutes of labour. The wage rate is £8.40 per hour. The sales of the product are anticipated to be:

	April	May	June	July
Sales units	7,200	7,050	6,550	6,150

OP-ST 1000 *May*
CL-ST 900

The product is produced one month prior to sale and wages are paid in the month of production. Inventory (stock) levels of finished goods are to remain at 1,000 units until the end of May when they will be reduced to 900 units and reduced further to 750 units at the end of June.

Complete the following

	April	May	June
Budgeted cash wages payments (£)			

Task 5.7

Recent actual and estimated sales figures are as follows.

				£
	JUL	*AUG*	*SEP*	*JUN*
April (actual)	*96,000*	*99840*	*97920*	420,000
May (actual)	*192 000*	*200000*	*208 000*	400,000
June (estimate)	*100,000*	*120000*	*125000*	480,000
July (estimate)	*50 400*	*48,000*	*57600*	500,000
August (estimate)	*438400*	*667840*	*488520*	520,000
September (estimate)				510,000

All sales are on credit and the payment pattern is as follows.

20% pay in the month of sale after taking a 4% settlement discount

40% pay in the month following the sale

25% pay two months after the month of sale

12% pay three months after the month of sale

There are expected to be 3% irrecoverable (bad) debts.

The purchases of the business are all on credit and it is estimated that the following purchases will be made.

				£
	JUL	*AUG*	*SEP*	
May	*96000*	*112000*	*170,000*	250,000
June	*150 000*	*144,000*	*168.000*	240,000
July				280,000
August	*246,000*	*256,000*	*288.000*	300,000
September				310,000

40% of purchases are paid for in the month after the purchase has been made and the remainder are paid for two months after the month of purchase.

Wages are expected to be £60,000 each month and are paid in the month in which they are incurred. General overheads are anticipated to be a monthly £50,000 for June and July increasing to £55,000 thereafter. 75% of the general overheads are paid in the month in which they are incurred and the remainder in the following month. The general overheads figure includes a depreciation charge of £6,000 each month.

Selling expenses are expected to be 10% of the monthly sales value and are paid for in the month following the sale.

The business has planned to purchase new equipment for £42,000 in August and in the same month to dispose of old equipment with estimated sales proceeds of £7,500.

Overdraft interest is charged at 1% per month based on the overdraft balance at the start of the month. At 1 July it is anticipated that the business will have an overdraft of £82,000.

Complete the cash budget for July, August and September.

	July £	August £	September £
Cash receipts:			
Sales	438400	467840	488520
Proceeds from sale of equipment	0	7500	0
Cash payments:			
Purchases	246.000	256.000	288000
Wages	60,000	60,000	60,000
Overheads	44.000	47750	49,000
Selling expenses	48000	50000	52000
Equipment	0	42000	0
Overdraft interest	820	424	233
Total payments	398.820	456174	449233
Net cash flow for the month	39.580	19166	39287
Opening balance	(82,000)	(42420)	(23254)
Closing balance	(42420)	(23254)	16033

Task 5.8

An organisation operates in a highly seasonal sector of the retail industry. The company's management is estimating its cash requirements for the third quarter of the year, for which the following schedule of anticipated inflows and outflows has been produced by the sales and purchases departments.

Month	Sales	Purchases
	£	£
May	160,000	240,000
June	320,000	60,000
July	80,000	40,000
August	80,000	120,000
September	160,000	180,000
October	220,000	120,000
November	180,000	80,000

Sales are made on two months' credit, whilst suppliers allow one month's credit. Monthly salaries amount to £36,000 and the company's annual rent of £48,000 is paid quarterly in advance.

An overdraft of £112,000 is expected to exist on 30 June.

Complete the cash budget for July, August and September.

	July	August	September
	£'000	£'000	£'000
Cash receipts:			
Sales	160	320	80
Cash payments:			
Purchases	60	40	120
Salaries	36	36	36
Rent	12	0	0
Total payments	108	76	156
Net cash flow for the month	52	244	(76)
Opening balance	(112)	(60)	184
Closing balance	(60)	184	108

Task 5.9

A manufacturing business is to prepare its cash budget for the three months ending 31 December. The business manufactures a single product which requires 3 kg of raw material per unit and 3 hours of labour per unit. Production takes place in the month of sale. The raw material cost is anticipated to be £9 per kg and the labour force are paid at a rate of £7.20 per hour. Each unit of the product sells for £75.

OCT   NOV   DEC
153.000 162000 174000
225000 229500 243000
378000 391500 417000

The forecast sales in units are as follows.

	August	September	October	November	December
	375,000	*382500*	*405000*	*435000*	*450000*
Forecast sales – units	5,000	5,100	5,400	5,800	6,000

Sales are on credit with 40% of receivables (debtors) paying the month after sale and the remainder two months after the sale.

Inventory (stock) of completed units is anticipated to be 500 until the start of October but this is to be increased by 100 units each month at the end of October, November and December.

The raw materials required for production are purchased in the month prior to production and 60% are paid for in the following month and the remainder two months after purchase. The anticipated inventory (stock) of raw materials is 3,000 kgs until the end of September and the planned inventory (stock) levels at the end of each month thereafter are as follows:

OCT   NOV   DEC

October	*89100* *96660* *100440*	3,200 kgs
November	*55080* *59400* *64440*	3,500 kgs
December		4,000 kgs

Wages are paid in the month in which they are incurred.

Production overheads are expected to be £60,000 each month and are paid for in the month in which they are incurred. This figure includes depreciation of £10,000 per month for machinery. General overheads are anticipated to be £72,000 each month in October and November increasing to £80,000 in December and are paid in the month in which they are incurred. The figure for general overheads includes £12,000 of depreciation each month.

The cash balance at 1 October is expected to be £40,000 in credit.

Complete the cash budget for October, November and December.

	October	November	December
	£	£	£
Cash receipts:			
Sales	*378.000*	*391500*	*417000*
Cash payments:			
Purchases	*144180*	*156060*	*164880*
Wages	*118800*	*127440*	*131760*
Production overheads	*50,000*	*50000*	*50000*
General overheads	*60000*	*60000*	*68000*
Total payments	*372980*	*393500*	*414640*
Net cash flow for the month	*5020*	*(2000)*	*2360*
Opening balance	40,000	*45020*	*43020*
Closing balance	*45020*	*43020*	*45380*

Task 5.10

A manufacturing business has the following extracts from its budgeted statement of financial position and its budgeted income statement for the following year 20X5, along with the actual balances and results for 20X4.

Statement of financial position

	As at 31 December 20X4 £	As at 31 December 20X5 £
Receivables (debtors)	23,000	19,000
Payables (creditors)	5,600	12,800

The payables relate only to supplies of materials.

Income statement

	Y/e 31 December 20X4 £	Y/e 31 December 20X5 £
Sales	240,300	228,400
Materials purchases	120,000	128,000

Calculate the cash flows in respect of sales and purchases.

OP. DEBTORS 23,000   OP. CR. 5600
SALES 228,400   PURCH 128000
CL. DEBTORS 19,000   CL.CR. 12800
INFLOW 232,400   OUTFLOW 120 800

STOCK KGS
	AUG	SEP	OCT	NOV	DEC
	3000	3000	3000	3200	3500
SALE	15300	16500	17700	18300	
	3000	3000	3200	3500	4000
PRCH	15300	16500	17900	13600	18800
	x9	x9	x9	x9	
	137,700	148500	161100	167400	

PROD
	AUG	SEP	OCT	NOV	DEC
OP.ST.	(500)	(500)	(500)	(600)	(700)
SALES	5000	5100	5400	5800	6000
CL.ST.	500	500	600	700	800
PROD	5000	5100	5500	5900	6100
	108000	110160	118800	127440	131760

Chapter 6

Task 6.1

A business has budgeted sales demand of 12,000 units in the coming month.

Each unit requires 2kg of material. 24,000 kgs ✓

Each unit requires 0.5 machine hours. 6000 HRS

Each unit requires 1.5 labour hours. 18000 HRS ✓

The availability of resource for the coming period is as follows:

Raw material available = 25,000 kg ✓

There are five machines each capable of operating for 1,000 hours 5000 HRS

There are 40 workers each capable of operating for 500 hours 20000 HRS ✓

No inventory (stock) of finished goods or raw materials is kept.

What is the limiting factor in the budget?

Select from:

- Sales demand
- Material
- Machine hours
- Labour hours

. . . .

Task 6.2

A business makes a single product, each unit of which requires 5 kgs of raw material. Unfortunately, due to a shortage of suppliers of the raw material, only 129,000 kgs will be available in the coming year. The materials are available on a monthly basis spread evenly over the year.

Complete the following:

The number of units that can be produced in total is ...... 25800 ......

The number of units that can be produced each month is ...... 2150 ......

. . . .

Task 6.3

The raw materials requirements for production for the next six months for a business are as follows:

	July	Aug	Sept	Oct	Nov	Dec
Raw materials requirements – kg	4,800	4,300	4,100	4,900	4,200	5,000

It is only possible to purchase 4,500 kg of the product each month.

Complete the following to show the maximum shortage of raw materials over the six-month period, monthly and in total, if only the amount required (up to the maximum allowed) is purchased each month.

	July	Aug	Sept	Oct	Nov	Dec
Requirement	4800	4300	4100	4900	4200	5000
Purchase	4500	4300	4100	4500	4200	4500
Shortfall	300	0	0	400	0	500

1200

Complete the following to show how many kgs of the material should be purchased each month in order to maximise production and keep inventory (stock) levels to the minimum possible. Give the total shortage of raw materials over the six-month period under this policy.

	July	Aug	Sept	Oct	Nov	Dec
Requirement	4800	4300	4100	4900	4200	5000
Purchase	4500	4500	4500	4500	4500	4500
Excess/(Shortfall)	(300)	200	400	(400)	300	(450)
Inventory (stock)	—	200	600			
Production	4500	4300	4100			

Task 6.4

How could a business try to alleviate the problem of shortage of materials if:

(a) the shortage is a short-term problem and full supplies will be available after a few months; or

(b) the shortage is a long-term problem?

Task 6.5

The raw materials requirements for production for Selby Electronics for the next six months are as follows:

	May	June	July	Aug	Sep	Oct
Raw materials requirements – kg	9,500	10,200	10,200	9,300	10,200	10,300

Selby is only able to purchase 10,000 kgs of the material in each month.

Complete the following which schedules the purchases in order to ensure the maximum production over the six-month period together with the minimum possible inventory (stock) level. Give the level of shortages under this purchasing scheme.

	May	June	July	Aug	Sep	Oct
Requirement						
Potential shortage						
Purchases						
Inventory (stock)						
Production						

Task 6.6

A product requires three hours of skilled labour per unit but there are only 12 such employees. They normally work a 38-hour week although, by paying an overtime rate of double time, it has been possible to negotiate for each employee to work eight hours of overtime a week.

The maximum level of production each week is ....184...

Other ways of solving the labour shortage problem are:

Task 6.7

Next week the sales demand is expected to be for 1,860 units. Each unit requires four hours of direct labour time and there are 160 employees each working a 35-hour week.

What is the overtime (in hours) required in order to meet demand with the current workforce?

Select from:

- 1,840
- 3,740
- 7,440
- 5,600

Handwritten working:

160 × 35 = 5600

1860 × 4 = 7440 HRS
        - 5600
        ─────
          1840

··

Task 6.8

There are two identical production lines in a factory. The factory operates two seven-hour shifts each day for five days a week with the production lines working at full capacity. The production line is capable of producing 30 units of product per hour.

The maximum production for a week is ....2100....

If sales demand were to exceed the maximum production level, the options would be .....extra shift, lengthen shift, open 6-7 days.....
......Speed up production line.

··

Task 6.9

Give three examples of possible key budget factors for a manufacturing organisation other than sales demand. MAT, LAB, MACHINE CAPACITY

··

Task 6.10

In each of the following situations, suggest what may be the key budget factor:

	Key budget factor
A private nursing home with 140 beds. The home is situated in an area which has a large proportion of retired amongst the population and there is little difficulty in recruiting suitable staff.	BEDS
A vendor of ice cream in a busy shopping centre. The transportable stall can store a maximum of 50 litres of ice cream.	Capacity
A partnership of three skilled craftsmen making carved chess sets from wood and marble for home sales and exports to specific order. Sales demand is high and orders have to be frequently rejected.	LABOUR Hours
A manufacturer of CD players and hi-fi systems which are similar to those of other manufacturers and who distributes the systems amongst a number of small high street electrical retailers.	SALES DEMAND

Task 6.11

Four products have the following sales price and resource requirements.

	W	X	Y	Z
Sales price £.	200	90	180	150
Materials (kg)	20 60	8 24	19 57	12 36
Labour (hours)	4 24	5 30	12 72	6 36
Maximum demand	300	1500	400	1000

The material costs £3 per kg. $\frac{116}{20}$

Cost of labour is £6 per hour. £5·80

$\frac{36}{8}$ £4·50

$\frac{51}{19}$ £2·68

$\frac{78}{12}$ £6·50

Materials are restricted to 20,000 kg.

12,000 kN

Complete the production schedule

	Production units
Product W 300 × 20 = 6600)	300
Product X _ 2000/8	250
Product Y 00 kg	330
Product Z 12000 kg	1000

Chapter 7

Task 7.1

The budget for production supervisors' costs for a period at an activity level of 250,000 units is £15,000. One production supervisor is required for every 100,000 units of production.

If actual production is 330,000 units what figure would appear in the flexed budget for production supervisors' costs?

Select from:

▪ £60,000

▪ £20,000

▪ £15,000

▪ £19,800

Task 7.2

	100,000 units	120,000 units
	£	£
Materials cost	240,000	288,000
Labour cost	124,000	144,000
Production overhead	38,000	38,000

The costs which would appear in a budget flexed to an actual activity level of 112,000 units would be:

Material cost ....

Labour cost ....

Production overhead ....

Task 7.3

The budgeted production overhead for a business is £524,000 at an activity level of 60,000 units and £664,000 at an activity level of 80,000 units.

If the actual activity level is 72,000 units, the flexed budget figure for production overhead is ....

Task 7.4

Complete the following flexed budget, given the following details of the cost behaviour of each of the costs.

Materials	the materials cost is totally variable
Labour	each operative can only produce 2,000 units each quarter – the cost of each operative is £3,500 each quarter
Production overhead	the production overhead is a totally fixed cost
General expenses	the general expenses are made up of a budgeted fixed cost of £6,400 and a variable element

Actual sales and production were in fact only 15,000 units during quarter 4. Prepare a flexed budget for an activity level of 15,000 units.

	Budget	Flexed budget
	20,000 units	15,000 units
	£	£
Sales (20,000 units)	130,000	
Material	(55,000)	
Labour	(35,000)	
Production overhead	(18,000)	
Gross profit	22,000	
General expenses	12,000	
Operating profit	10,000	

Task 7.5

Complete both the tables to show the variances of actual performance against budget, and then actual performance against flexed budget. Comment on the differences in variances under the two tables.

	Budget	Actual	Variances
	28,000 units	31,500 units	
	£	£	£
Sales	406,000	441,000	
Materials	165,200	180,400	
Labour	100,800	115,600	
Production overhead	37,500	39,000	_____
Gross profit	102,500	106,000	
General expenses	55,600	68,900	_____
Operating profit	46,900	37,100	_____

The materials and labour costs are variable costs, the production overhead is a fixed cost and the general expenses are a semi-variable cost with a fixed element of £13,600

	Flexed budget	Actual	Variances
	31,500 units	31,500 units	
	£	£	£
Sales		441,000	
Materials		180,400	
Labour		115,600	
Production overhead	_____	39,000	_____
Gross profit		106,000	
General expenses	_____	68,900	_____
Operating profit	_____	37,100	_____

Reason for difference in variances:

....

Task 7.6

Given below is the original fixed budget for a manufacturing operation for quarter 2. However, as sales and production were subsequently anticipated to be higher than this budget made allowance for, a revised budget was also prepared. The actual results for quarter 2 are also given.

	Original budget 200,000 units		Revised budget 240,000 units		Actual 230,000 units	
	£	£	£	£	£	£
Sales		1,360,000		1,632,000		1,532,000
Materials	690,000		828,000		783,200	
Labour	387,000		449,000		428,600	
Production						
Expenses	162,000		186,000		173,500	
Production cost		1,239,000		1,463,000		1,385,300
Gross profit		121,000		169,000		146,700
General						
Expenses		72,000		72,000		74,700
Operating profit		49,000		97,000		72,000

Complete the following flexed budget to reflect the actual level of activity for the quarter, and calculate the variances from that budget.

	Flexed budget units		Actual units		Variances
	£	£	£	£	£
Sales				1,532,000	
Materials			783,200		
Labour			428,600		
Production expenses	___		173,500		
Production cost		___		1,385,300	
Gross profit				146,700	
General expenses		___		74,700	
Operating profit		___		72,000	

Task 7.7

Given below is the budget for quarter 2 prepared using absorption costing principles. There was no opening inventory (stock).

	Quarter 2 budget	
	£	£
Sales (50,000 units)		400,000
Materials	165,400	
Labour	69,800	
Production overhead	56,000	
Cost of production		
56,000 units	291,200	
Less: closing inventory (stock)	31,200	
Cost of sales		260,000
Gross profit		140,000
General expenses		52,000
Operating profit		88,000

The materials and labour costs are variable with the level of production but the production overhead and general expenses are both fixed costs.

Complete the following budget for quarter 2 using marginal costing principles, and reconcile the budgeted profit figure using absorption costing to the budgeted profit figure using marginal costing.

	£	£
Sales 50,000 units		
Materials		
Labour		
Cost of production: 56,000 units		
Less: closing inventory (stock)		
Cost of sales		
Contribution		
Production overhead		
General expenses		
Operating profit		

	£
Profit per absorption costing budget	88,000
Profit per marginal costing budget	

Task 7.8

A business's sales director unexpectedly resigns during the year.

What effect might this have on variances?

Task 7.9

Due to the sudden illness of the credit controller, the credit control function is outsourced to an external agency during the year.

What effect might this have on variances?

Task 7.10

Why is it important that managerial performance is only judged on the basis of controllable variances?

Task 7.11

Explain what is meant by feedback and feedforward.

Task 7.12

Given below is the original fixed budget and the actual results for the same period.

	Budget		Actual	
Units	30,000		34,000	
	£	£	£	£
Sales		660,000		697,000
Direct costs				
Materials	252,000		299,200	
Labour	180,000		192,600	
Factory power	83,600		88,600	
	515,600		580,400	
Fixed overheads	75,000		79,000	
Cost of sales		590,600		659,400
Operating profit		69,400		37,600

You are also provided with the following information:

(i)   There is no inventory (stock) of finished goods

(ii) The production employees are paid per week irrespective of the production level. The employees that were budgeted for are capable of producing a maximum of 45,000 units in a six-month period

(iii) The budgeted and actual figures for factory power include a fixed cost element of £20,600

Prepare a report for the Chief Executive including the following:

A flexed operating statement for the actual activity level using marginal costing principles, calculating the variances for the sales and costs figures, as set out below.

An explanation of why the flexed budget operating statement shows different results from that of the original budget.

Units	Flexed budget 34,000		Actual 34,000		Variance
	£	£	£	£	£
Sales					
Direct costs					
Materials					
Factory power					
	———		———		
		———		———	
Contribution					
Labour					
Factory power					
Fixed overheads	———		———		
Fixed costs		———		———	
Operating profit		═══		═══	

Task 7.13

An original budget, revised budget and actual costs are shown for a period below, along with variances from the revised budget.

Budgeted and actual costs

	Original budget	Revised budget	Actual results	Variances from revised budget
Production and sales (units)	24,000	20,000	22,000	2,000 (F)
	£	£	£	£
Variable costs				
Material	216,000	180,000	206,800	26,800 (A)
Labour	288,000	240,000	255,200	15,200 (A)
Semi-variable costs				
Heat, light and power	31,000	27,000	33,400	6,400 (A)
Fixed costs				
Rent, rates and depreciation	40,000	40,000	38,000	2,000 (F)
	575,000	487,000	533,400	46,400 (A)

Assumptions in the two budgets
1   No change in input prices
2   No change in the quantity of variable inputs per unit of product output

One invoice for heat, light and power for £7,520 had been incorrectly coded. The invoice should have been coded to materials.

Complete the following flexed budget and variances, after correcting for the miscoded invoice.

	Flexed budget	Actual	Variance £
	22,000 units	22,000 units	
Production and sales units			
Variable costs:	£	£	
Material			
Labour			
Semi-variable costs			
Heat, light, power			
Fixed costs:			
Rent, rates, depreciation			
Total costs			

The revised budget was set using a participative approach to budgeting, used to try to motivate staff.

Give two reasons why favourable cost variances may arise, other than due to better cost control.

Give two reasons why higher sales volume may not be the result of improved motivation due to the introduction of participative budgeting.

Task 7.14

A business makes a CD player that is fitted to the cars made by its parent company.

You have the following information.

- Two draft budgets for the coming year. The first assumes a production and sales volume of 80,000 CD players. The second assumes a production and sales volume of 100,000 CD players. Any differences between the two budgets arose entirely from the different volumes assumed.

- The actual operating results for the year.

- A note stating there was no opening or closing inventory (stock) of any sort.

- A note stating that there were no purchases or sales of non-current (fixed) assets during the year.

The draft budgets and actual results from the working papers are shown below.

Budgets and actual results						
	Draft budgets				**Actual results**	
CD player production and sales volume	80,000		100,000		140,000	
	£'000	£'000	£'000	£'000	£'000	£'000
Conversion costs						
Labour	640		760		972	
Light, heat and power	370		450		586	
Rent, rates and insurance	200		200		200	
Depreciation	150		150		132	
		1,360		1,560		1,890
Bought-in materials		1,600		2,000		3,220
Total expense		2,960		3,560		5,110
Revenue (turnover)		3,200		4,000		6,440
Operating profit		240		440		1,330

Complete the following flexed budget statement showing the budgeted and actual results and any variances.

	Flexed budget	Actual results	Variances
Production and sales volume (CD players)	140,000	140,000	
	£'000	£'000	£'000
Conversion costs			
Labour		972	
Light, heat and power		586	
Rent, rates and insurance		200	
Depreciation	_____	132	
Total conversion costs		1,890	

	Flexed budget	Actual results	Variances
Bought-in materials	_____	3,220	
Total expenses		5,110	
Revenue (turnover)	_____	6,440	
Operating profit	=========	1,330	

The Chief Executive believes the high profits of £1,330,000 are due to increased effort by the managers following the introduction of performance related pay at the beginning of this year. Details of the scheme are:

- The bought-in materials for the CD players are purchased from outside suppliers but the conversion costs – those manufacturing costs that transform the raw materials into the finished product – are all provided the company.

- The only customer for the CD player is the parent company. Because of this, there is no market price and so the price has had to be negotiated.

- It was agreed that the price of the CD players sold to the parent company should be twice the cost of the bought-in materials.

- Additional performance related payments are based on the following.

    - Exceeding the annual budgeted volume of sales

    - Increasing the actual profit per CD player above the budgeted profit per CD player

- The budgeted sales volume for the year was 100,000 CD players and the budgeted profit per CD player was £4.40.

- The actual sales volume for the year was 140,000 and the actual profit per CD player was £9.50.

Write a memo to the Chief Executive, which covers the following:

Use the data in the question to explain THREE reasons why profits might have improved even without the introduction of performance related pay.

Identify THREE general conditions necessary for performance related pay to lead to improved performance.

∎∎∎

Chapter 8

Task 8.1

Suggest suitable non-financial performance indicators to compare budgeted versus actual performance for an online clothes shop.

Task 8.2

Suggest possible measures of productivity for each of the following types of organisation:

- a vet's surgery
- a bar
- a firm of solicitors
- a retail store
- a wedding-cake business

Task 8.3

A component is made by the manual operation of a number of cutting machines. The process produces shavings of material which are collected each day, and stored until removed by a rubbish collection service.

What performance measures or indicators will be useful to the production manager with regard to material?

Task 8.4

At an accountancy firm, trainees spend part of their time at college, and part in the office. What performance measures will be useful for the Office Managing Partner in relation to trainees?

Task 8.5

A business uses a small number of large machines, which are only replaced every 20 years.

What are useful performance measures relating to the machines?

Task 8.6

Suggest performance indicators to measure customer service by a restaurant.

Task 8.7

A bus company collects the following information in order to monitor performance.

- Number of drivers
- Number of passengers
- Number of miles travelled
- Number of journeys undertaken
- Maintenance costs

This information is known over any time period.

- **Suggest measures that could be used to compare budgeted and actual performance in order to monitor the following performance indicators:**
- **Driver productivity**
- **Satisfaction of passenger needs indicators, using the information collected**
- **Satisfaction of passenger needs indicators, which would require other information**
- **Safety indicators, using existing information**
- **Safety indicators, requiring other information**

Answer bank

Answer bank

Chapter 1

Task 1.1

Cost	Budget
Market research survey	Marketing budget
Wages of factory workers	Production budget
Recruitment advertisement for a new finance director in an accountancy magazine	Administrative overheads budget
Raw material costs	Production budget
Salary of marketing director	Marketing budget

Task 1.2

Function	Department
Prepares accounting information, pays suppliers and staff, chases customers for payment etc	Finance department
Recruits, develops and disciplines staff, and ensures that employment law is followed by the business	HR department
Buys raw materials for use in the production process	Purchasing team
Makes sales to new and existing customers	Sales team
Investigates and responds to customer complaints	After-sales service team

Task 1.3

Cost	Behaviour
Room hire	Fixed
Food for attendees	Variable
Hire of waiting staff – 1 required per 20 attendees	Stepped

Answer bank

Task 1.4

True ☑

False ☐

Workings

	20,000 units	32,000 units
Total cost	£128,000	£204,800
Cost per unit	£6.40	£6.40

Therefore this is a variable cost as cost per unit is the same at each activity level.

....

Task 1.5

Heating	Floor area
Rental on storage unit for raw materials held	Average inventory (stock) of raw materials
Canteen expenses	Number of staff employed
Depreciation of factory building	Floor area

....

Task 1.6

	Cost behaviour
Cost 1	Fixed
Cost 2	Stepped
Cost 3	Variable
Cost 4	Semi-variable

....

Task 1.7

Activity level (units)	Budgeted total production cost £	Budgeted cost per unit £
8,000	33,400	4.175
12,000	42,600	3.550
15,000	49,500	3.300

Workings

	8,000 units	12,000 units	15,000 units
	£	£	£
Variable costs			
£23,000/10,000 x 8,000	18,400		
£23,000/10,000 x 12,000		27,600	
£23,000/10,000 x 15,000			34,500
Fixed costs	15,000	15,000	15,000
	33,400	42,600	49,500
Cost per unit	£4.175	£3.55	£3.30

Task 1.8

	Cost behaviour
Maintenance contract which costs £10,000 annually plus an average of £500 cost per call out	Semi-variable
Sales car depreciation based on miles travelled	Variable
Machine consumables cost based on machine hours	Variable
Rent for a building that houses the factory, stores and maintenance departments	Fixed

Task 1.9

Costs	Accounting treatment
Servicing of office computer equipment	Allocate to administrative overheads
Materials wastage in production process	Direct cost
Depreciation of marketing director's car	Allocate to marketing overheads
Bonus for finance director	Allocate to administrative overheads
Sick pay for production workers	Charge to production in a labour hour overhead rate

Task 1.10

(i) **Absorption costing**

Apportionment of overheads

	Cutting	Finishing	Stores
	£	£	£
Allocated overhead	380,000	280,000	120,000
Stores overhead apportioned 80:20	96,000	24,000	(120,000)
	476,000	304,000	–

Hours worked	50,000 x 3	150,000	
	50,000 x 2		100,000

Overhead absorption rate

$$\frac{476,000}{150,000} = £3.17 \text{ per labour hour} \qquad \frac{304,000}{100,000} = £3.04 \text{ per labour hour}$$

Unit cost – absorption costing

	£
Direct materials	16.00
Labour – cutting 3 hours x £7.50	22.50
finishing 2 hours x £6.80	13.60
Overheads – cutting 3 hours x £3.17	9.51
finishing 2 hours x £3.04	6.08
Unit cost	67.69

(ii) **Marginal costing**

Unit cost – marginal costing

	£
Direct materials	16.00
Labour – cutting 3 hours x £7.50	22.50
finishing 2 hours x £6.80	13.60
Cutting £380,000 x 60%/50,000	4.56
Finishing £280,000 x 60%/50,000	3.36
Stores £120,000 x 60%/50,000	1.44
Unit cost	61.46

Task 1.11

(a)

	£
Fixed production costs absorbed by the product	41,250
Over/under absorption of fixed product costs	3,750

The fixed production overhead absorbed by the products would be 16,500 units produced x £2.50 (W2) = £41,250.

Budgeted annual fixed production overhead (W1) = £150,000

	£
Actual quarterly fixed production o/hd = budgeted quarterly prod'n o/hd (£150,000/4)	37,500
Production o/hd absorbed into production (see above)	41,250
Over absorption of fixed production o/hd	3,750

(b) **Profit for the quarter, using absorption costing**

	£	£	£
Sales (13,500 × £12) (W3)			162,000
Costs of production (no opening inventory (stock))			
Value of inventory (stock) produced (16,500 × £8.50) (W2)		140,250	
Less value of closing inventory (stock) ((16,500 – 13,500) units × full production cost of £8.50) (W2)		(25,500)	
Total cost of production			(114,750)
			47,250
Selling, distribution & admin costs			
Variable (13,500 × £1)(W1)		13,500	
Fixed (¼ of £90,000)(W1)		22,500	
Total selling, distribution & admin costs			(36,000)
			11,250
add **over-absorbed** production overhead (a)			3,750
Absorption costing profit			15,000

(c) **Profit statement using marginal costing**

	£	£
Sales		162,000
Variable costs of production (16,500 × £6) (W1)	99,000	
Less value of closing inventory (stock) (3,000 × £6) (W1)	(18,000)	
Variable cost of sales	81,000	
Variable selling, distribution & admin costs (13,500 × £1) (W1)	13,500	
Total variable costs (13,500 × £7)		94,500
Contribution (13,500 × £5)		67,500
Fixed costs: production (£150,000/4)	37,500	
selling, distribution & admin (£90,000/4)	22,500	
Total fixed costs		(60,000)
Marginal costing profit		7,500

Workings

(1)

	Production costs	Selling, dist & admin costs
Using Hi Lo method:	£	£
Total costs of 60,000 units (fixed plus variable)	510,000	150,000
Total costs of 36,000 units (fixed plus variable)	366,000	126,000
Difference = variable costs of 24,000 units	144,000	24,000
Variable costs per unit	£6	£1
	Production costs	Selling, dist & admin costs
	£	£
Total costs of 60,000 units	510,000	150,000
Variable costs of 60,000 units (x £6 or £1)	(360,000)	(60,000)
Fixed costs	150,000	90,000

(2) The rate of absorption of fixed production overheads will therefore be:

$$\frac{£150,000}{60,000} = £2.50 \text{ per unit}$$

Total absorption costing production cost = £(6 + 2.50) = £8.50

(3) Selling price: £432,000/36,000 units = £12 (or £720,000/60,000)

- -

Task 1.12

File note

To: Drampton's finance director

From: Financial analyst

Date: xx/xx/xx

Subject: **Little Ltd – treatment of fixed overheads**

Following our recent discussions, I set out below calculations showing the reclassification of fixed overheads between the two units manufactured by Little Ltd, using activity-based costing.

	Allocated overheads to Server £	Allocated overheads to PC £
Set-up costs	10,000	-
Rent & power (production area)	24,000	96,000
Rent (stores area)	25,000	25,000
Salaries of store issue staff	8,000	32,000

Step 1. Calculation of cost per cost driver

	Budgeted total annual overheads £	Cost driver	Number of cost drivers	Cost per Cost driver £
Set-up costs	10,000	Number of set-ups	5	2,000.00
Rent and power (production area)	120,000	Number of wks' production	50	2,400.00
Rent (stores area)	50,000	Floor area of stores (m^2)	800	62.50
Salaries of store issue staff	40,000	No of issues of stock	10,000	4.00
	220,000			

Step 2. Reallocation of overheads based on costs per cost driver

Server

	(i) *Number of cost drivers*	(ii) *Cost per cost driver* £	(i) × (ii) *Allocated overheads*
Set-up costs	5	2,000.00	10,000
Rent & power (production area)	10	2,400.00	24,000
Rent (stores area)	400	62.50	25,000
Salaries of store issue staff	2,000	4.00	8,000
			67,000

PC

	(i) *Number of cost drivers*	(ii) *Cost per cost driver* £	(i) × (ii) *Allocated overheads*
Set-up costs	0	2,000.00	–
Rent and power (production area)	40	2,400.00	96,000
Rent (stores area)	400	62.50	25,000
Salaries of store issue staff	8,000	4.00	32,000
			153,000

....

Chapter 2

Task 2.1

A budget is a formalised, numerical plan of action for all areas of a business for the forthcoming period, normally set for the next twelve-month period.

A budgetary control system can help management to perform their duties in two main areas.

One of the roles of management is in terms of planning for the business – both long term strategic plans and shorter term operational plans. Budgets are formal, numerical plans which can help to ensure that all areas of the business are aiming at the same goals.

For example, once the sales and manufacturing budgets are set, management can then ensure that the budgets for other areas of the business such as the canteen and the sales department are in line with these budgets. So, for example, if it is budgeted that there will be 200 factory workers each day then the canteen should not be budgeting to buy food for 400. Or if sales are expected to be 60,000 units in the period it is important that the sales department budgets in order to be able to deal with this level.

A further important role of management is that of control of operations and of costs in particular. A budgetary system can assist in this area as the eventual actual results can be compared to the budgeted figures and any variances can be calculated and investigated. Where necessary management can then take corrective action to deal with these variances from planned costs.

Task 2.2

Scenario	Budget use
The managing director reduces the figure in next year's budget for the staff Christmas party by 25%	Control
The sales director divides the costs for client entertainment between his two sales teams, and gives the managers of those teams permission to spend within that level	Authorisation
A bonus cost of 2% of sales is included in the sales team's budget for the coming period	Motivation
A retail company is wishing to expand its operations and so includes the rental costs of new shops in its budget	Planning
The purchasing manager informs the production manager there will be a world-wide shortage of material in the coming period. The production manager budgets for a different product mix because of this.	Co-ordination

Task 2.3

Strategic and operational plans

The strategic plans of a business are the long-term plans of the business. These plans will be based upon the strategic objectives of the management of the business which may concern maximisation of profitability, increase of market share, growth by acquisition of other businesses or expansion of the product range. Once the strategic objectives have been determined, then the strategic plans are the long term plans of how the business is to meet these objectives.

Once the strategic plan is in place then the management can look at shorter term plans necessary in order to meet the strategic objectives of the business. These are the operational plans and will take a variety of forms such as plans for the purchase of fixed assets, plans for the amount of production and plans for the financing of the business. All of these plans take the form of budgets.

Setting of strategic and operational plans

When a business is started the management must determine a long-term plan of how the business is to be operated and where its future lies. This will mean that the senior management of the business must determine the strategic objectives of the business. The strategic plan will remain in place for the life of the business but may be altered from time to time as circumstances change or opportunities become available.

The strategic plan shows where the business is going but the next stage of the planning process is to determine how the business is going to get there. This will involve a detailed review of the business both from an internal and external perspective in order to decide what possible strategies there are in order to move the business closer to the strategic objective.

Information will need to be gathered about all of the resources of the business, the state of its products or services and the amount of finance that is available. External information about the market, competitors and the general economic environment will also be required. This detailed review of the position of the business is often called a SWOT analysis, a review of the strengths, weaknesses, opportunities and threats to the business.

Once this analysis has been carried out, management will be in a position to identify the various strategies that are available to the organisation, such as marketing a new product or concentrating on the production of its current products.

Once the various available strategies have been identified then the management will be in a position to choose which strategy is the most suitable and has the greatest potential for achieving the overall strategic objective. When the strategies for the future have been chosen then they can be co-ordinated into the strategic plan for the business.

Once the strategic plan is in place then the management can look at shorter term plans necessary in order to meet the strategies chosen for the business, the operational plans.

Tutorial note: this task (and many of the others in this chapter) has been included to help you learn about and understand the planning process in a business, but the answer is more detailed than any you would be expected to give in the assessment.

Task 2.4

Budget manual

The budget manual is a set of detailed instructions as to how the budget is to be prepared. The budget manual might typically include the following:

- the names of the budget holders – those responsible for producing each budget
- to whom each budget holder reports
- an organisation chart
- the timescale for the production of each budget
- the procedures for preparing each budget
- the format of the budgets
- how and when actual performance is compared to budget

Budget committee

The budget committee is responsible for co-ordinating and administering all of the individual budgets and will review and authorise each individual budget. The budget committee will normally be made up of senior executives and each function of the business should be represented on the budget committee in order to ensure that there is full communication between all areas of the business. The budget committee will normally be assisted by an accountant known as the budget officer.

Budget holders

Budget holders are the managers within a business that are responsible for preparing each resource budget. In most cases the budget holder should be the manager who will also be responsible for ensuring that the activities meet the budget.

Master budget

The master budget is the final overall budget for all areas of the business. It is normally set out in the form of a budgeted profit and loss account, budgeted balance sheet and cash flow budget.

Task 2.5

Budgeting process

The budgeting process starts with the setting of the budget (forecast) for the key budget factor. This will frequently be the sales budget although, if manufacturing resources are the key budget factor, this may be the labour budget or machine hours budget. Once the key budget factor budget has been set then the production budget will be set by the production manager and the various other resource budgets set by the relevant budget holders.

Once the budget holder has drafted his budget then he will submit this to the budget committee. The budget officer will ensure that the budget is consistent with the other resource budgets, checking, for example, that it has been prepared in line with the production budget.

There will then frequently be negotiations between the budget committee and the budget holder regarding the detailed content of the budget. The manager might for example have built in an increase in costs over previous years which the budget committee does not agree with. The budget holder may well have to change his draft budget and re-submit it to the budget committee a number of times before the budget committee is satisfied with it.

Once the budget committee have agreed all of the resource budgets with the budget holders then they will be formed into the master budget.

Task 2.6

Rolling budget

A rolling budget is one which is constantly being updated and added to. It will be set in detail for the next short accounting period and in outline for the remainder of the 12-month period. As each accounting period passes, the details of the next period's budget are produced and the budget extended to maintain a 12-month coverage.

For example if budgets are set for each of 13 four-week periods in a year, initially the detailed budget will be set for period 1 and the remaining 12 periods' budgets will be in outline. Towards the end of period 1 the detail for period 2's budget will be set and the outline budget for period 1 of the following year added.

The benefits of a rolling budget are that the detailed budgeting only has to be performed for the next accounting period rather than for periods a long time in advance, therefore the budget is potentially more accurate. This makes it more useful to you when assessing the performance of the business by comparing actual results with the budgeted figures. It also means that when setting the detail of each period's budget, the budget holder can react to changes in circumstances that are revealed by comparison of the actual figures for each period to the budgeted figures.

Task 2.7

To: Managing Director

From: An Accountant

Subject: The budgeting process

Date: XX XX XX

The method of budgeting that is usually used may not be the most appropriate for the business.

Current method

The current method is incremental budgeting, as this takes the prior year budget and adjust the costs included for changes in price and level of output.

However, the activities of the business, and how these are carried out, may have changed significantly over recent years. For example, the production process may now use more advanced machinery, and less labour, leading to higher power, maintenance and depreciation costs, but lower labour costs. This means the costs may be out of date.

The current method of budgeting does not encourage costs savings or efficiencies, as inefficiencies and any budget slack are rolled forward year-on-year. As various costs are never kept within budget, with no apparent consequences, there is no motivation to stick to the budget.

Zero-based budgeting

An alternative would be to use zero-based budgeting. This looks at the costs of each cost centre from scratch for each period. Each cost is considered in the context of the production budget and the amount of each cost must then be specifically justified and not just included in the budget because it was in last year's budget.

For each item of activity which causes a cost, the following types of question must be asked:

- is the activity necessary?
- are there alternatives to this activity?
- what are the costs of the alternative?
- what would happen if the activity were not carried out?
- is the expense of the activity worth the benefit?

By asking such questions, the activity and its related costs can either be justified for inclusion in the budget or a cheaper alternative found.

Using this method would therefore promote cost-savings and efficiencies, eliminate budgetary slack and motivate staff as the budget is realistic, but challenging.

Chapter 3

Task 3.1

	Source
The previous year's financial statements for a company	Companies House
Previous month's discounts allowed	Internal accounting records
Industry average profit margin	Trade association
Information about a competitor's success	Financial press
Average sick days of employees per month	HR department

Task 3.2

Labour usage budget requires forecast production units and labour hours per unit

Task 3.3

Opening and closing inventory (stock) of raw materials.

(If the materials usage budget is already known, this will have already taken account of inventory (stock) of finished goods, and the production budget).

Task 3.4

A capital budget details the timing and value of the purchases of non-current (fixed) assets. This is important for a number of reasons.

- The purchase of non-current assets will normally be the most significant outgoing of a business and therefore it is important that such major purchases are properly planned.

- The purchase of non-current assets will normally be costly and it is therefore important that appropriate finance is available at the precise time that it is required.

- Non-current assets are frequently fundamental to the production and processes of an organisation therefore it is vital that non-current assets are fully functioning and are replaced or updated at the appropriate time.

Task 3.5

Resource budgets are those that deal with all aspects of the short term operations of the business. The resource budgets will include:

Production budget – this is a budget for the number of units that it is planned to produce during the forthcoming period – this will be based upon the key budget factor which is frequently the sales demand which will be forecast in the sales budget.

Materials usage budget – this is based upon the production budget and is a budget for the estimated quantity of materials that is to be used in the forthcoming period.

Materials purchases budget – this is the amount of raw materials that must be purchased each period to satisfy the production and inventory (stock) demands and will be expressed in both units and monetary amounts. These figures will be based upon the materials usage budget.

Labour usage budget – this is based upon the production budget and is an estimate of the labour hours required during the period to meet the production figures. The production budget will be the starting point for determining the labour usage budget.

Labour cost budget – this is based upon the labour usage budget and is the monetary cost of the labour hours required for the period, including any overtime.

Machine hours budget – this is based upon the production plans and shows the number of hours that the machinery must be working in order to produce the required level of production. The figures can be calculated using the quantity of production from the production budget.

Variable overheads budget – this will be based upon the production budget as the variable overheads will vary with the amount of production. Therefore the production budget will provide the quantities of production which can then be used to determine the variable overheads expected to be incurred.

Fixed overheads budget – this is independent of the level of production, as this should not affect the amount of fixed overheads. Therefore the budget for fixed overheads will be based upon estimates of fixed overhead costs and previous experience.

There may also be sundry other resource budgets such as the selling and distribution costs budget, advertising budget and the administration budget which will again all be set within the context of the sales budget.

Task 3.6

The general limitations of forecasting are:

- the less historical data that is used, the more unreliable the results of the forecast will be
- the further into the future that the forecast considers, the more unreliable it will become
- forecast figures will often be based upon the assumption that current conditions will continue in the future. A trend of results may be based upon historical data, but you cannot always assume that the trend will continue in the future
- if the forecast is based upon a trend, there are always random elements or variations which cause the trend to change

- the forecast produced from the historical data may be quite accurate but the actual future results may be very different from the forecast figures due to changes in the political, economic or technological environment within which the business operates

Task 3.7

Quarter 2	112,060 units
Quarter 3	136,262 units
Quarter 4	118,611 units

Workings

	Trend	Seasonal variation		Forecast
Quarter 2 ((122,000 – 6,000) x 1.035)	120,060	–8,000	=	112,060
Quarter 3 (120,060 x 1.035)	124,262	+12,000	=	136,262
Quarter 4 (124,262 x 1.035)	128,611	–10,000	=	118,611

Task 3.8

	Trend	Seasonal variation			Forecast
Quarter 1 (Trend = 335,000 + 5,000)	340,000	X	0.82	=	278,800
Quarter 2	345,000	X	1.21	=	417,450
Quarter 3	350,000	X	1.07	=	374,500
Quarter 4	355,000	X	0.90	=	319,500

Task 3.9

The main limitations of using time series analysis for forecasting are:

- unless the data used covers many years, it is impossible to isolate the cyclical changes due to general changes in the economy

- the seasonal variations are an average of the seasonal variation for each period and again, unless this is based on a large amount of historical data, the figure could be misleading

- any random variations are ignored

- the trend and the seasonal variations are assumed to continue in the future in the same manner as in the past

- if the time series analysis is based upon historic values, the figures will include past inflation which may not be an indication of the future amounts

Task 3.10

(a)

The product life cycle is generally thought to split into five separate stages:

- development
- launch
- growth
- maturity
- decline

During the development and launch stage of the product's life there are large outgoings in terms of development expenditure, non-current (fixed) assets necessary for production, the building up of inventory (stock) levels and advertising and promotion expenses. It is likely that even after the launch sales will be quite low and the product will be making a loss at this stage.

If the launch of the product is successful then during the growth stage there will be fairly rapid increases in sales and a move to profitability as the costs of the earlier stages are covered. However, these sales increases are not likely to continue indefinitely.

In the maturity stage of the product, demand for the product will probably start to slow down and become more constant. In many cases this is the stage where the product is modified or improved in order to sustain demand and this may then see a small surge in sales.

At some point in a product's life, unless it is a consumable item such as chocolate bars, the product will reach the end of its sale life, which is known as the decline stage. The market will have bought enough of the product and sales will decline. This is the point where the business should consider no longer producing the product.

(b) If the future demand for a product is to be forecast using time series analysis it is obviously important that the stage in the product life cycle that has been reached is taken into account. For example, if the trend is based upon the growth stage, whereas in fact the product is moving into the maturity stage, then the trend would show an overly optimistic forecast for sales.

Task 3.11

Maturity stage (because the pattern of sales is likely to be more constant).

Task 3.12

	Jan	Feb	Mar	Apr	May	Jun
Forecast variable production costs £ (production units x £10.50)	37,800	30,450	33,600	32,550	35,700	42,000
Forecast variable selling costs £ (sales units x £3.80)	13,300	11,400	11,400	12,160	13,300	14,440

Task 3.13

	Quarter 1	Quarter 2
Forecast direct materials costs £	667,396	722,633

Workings

Quarter 1	£657,000 x 128.4/126.4	=	£667,396
Quarter 2	£692,500 x 131.9/126.4	=	£722,633

Task 3.14

	Jan	Feb	Mar
Forecast variable production costs £	106,631	113,092	116,161
Forecast variable selling costs £	33,033	35,012	38,047

Variable production costs

		£
January	4,200 x £25 x 137.3/135.2	106,631
February	4,400 x £25 x 139.0/135.2	113,092
March	4,500 x £25 x 139.6/135.2	116,161

Variable selling costs

January	4,100 x £8 x 141.5/140.5	33,033
February	4,300 x £8 x 143.0/140.5	35,012
March	4,650 x £8 x 143.7/140.5	38,047

Task 3.15

The forecast total electricity, machinery maintenance and water costs for the coming month are £96,359.

		£
Electricity	£35,000 x 95% x 240.3/224.6	35,574
Maintenance costs	£20,000/4 x 2 x 1.05	10,500
Water costs	(£62,000 – 15,000) x 240.3/224.6	50,285
Total		96,359

Task 3.16

The forecast fixed costs for next year are £172,320

		£
Rent	£65,000 x 1.055	68,575
Insurance	£15,700 x 1.10	17,270
Power	£84,000 x 171.2/166.3	86,475
		172,320

The forecast fixed costs for next year are £ 172,320

Task 3.17

The estimated variable cost per machine hour is £15 per hour

	Machine hours	Cost £
June (lowest)	14,200	285,000
August (highest)	15,200	300,000
Increase	1,000	15,000

Variable cost = £15,000/1,000 hours
= £15 per hour

The estimated fixed costs of the maintenance department are £285,000

	£
June	
Variable element £15 x 14,200 hours	213,000
Fixed element (bal fig)	72,000
Total cost	285,000

The estimated variable cost per machine hour is £ 15 per hour

The estimated fixed costs of the maintenance department are £ 285,000

Task 3.18

Forecast units	Production costs £
74,000	685,000
90,000	797,000

Workings	Activity level	Cost £
July (lowest)	63,000	608,000
September (highest)	76,000	699,000
Increase	13,000	91,000
Variable element = £91,000/13,000		
= £7 per unit		

	£
July	
Variable element £7 x 63,000 units	441,000
Fixed element (bal fig)	167,000
Total cost	608,000

Production level of 74,000 units:

	£
Variable cost £7 x 74,000	518,000
Fixed cost	167,000
Total cost	685,000

Production level of 90,000 units:

	£
Variable cost £7 x 90,000	630,000
Fixed cost	167,000
Total cost	797,000

The estimate for the 74,000 units of production is likely to be more accurate than the estimate for 90,000 units. Estimating the costs at 74,000 units is an example of interpolation, in that the estimate is being made for a production level that is within the range of production levels used to estimate the variable and fixed costs. 90,000 units of production is significantly higher than the levels of production used in estimating fixed and variable costs and therefore it is possible that the costs would behave differently at this level of production. This is an example of extrapolation.

••

Task 3.19

a   =   the fixed element of the cost

b   =   the variable amount per unit/hour

••

Task 3.20

Production costs	=	138,000 + (6.4 x 105,000)
	=	£810,000

Task 3.21

Power costs:

	Machine hours	Power costs £
April	80,000 + (380,000 x 0.5)	270,000
May	80,000 + (400,000 x 0.5)	280,000
June	80,000 + (395,000 x 0.5)	277,500
July	80,000 + (405,000 x 0.5)	282,500
August	80,000 + (410,000 x 0.5)	285,000
September	80,000 + (420,000 x 0.5)	290,000

Task 3.22

	Sales trend (units)
Month 1	25,600
Month 2	26,500
Month 3	27,400

Workings

Month 1: sales trend	=	3.1 + 0.9 x 25 (month 25)
	=	25,600 units
Month 2: sales trend	=	3.1 + 0.9 x 26
	=	26,500 units
Month 3: sales trend	=	3.1 + 0.9 x 27
	=	27,400 units

Task 3.23

	Sales volume
Quarter 1	1,590
Quarter 2	2,095
Quarter 3	2,125
Quarter 4	1,880

Workings

	Trend		Seasonal variation		Estimate of sales
Quarter 1	400 + 105 x 13	=	1,765 – 175	=	1,590
Quarter 2	400 + 105 x 14	=	1,870 + 225	=	2,095
Quarter 3	400 + 105 x 15	=	1,975 + 150	=	2,125
Quarter 4	400 + 105 x 16	=	2,080 – 200	=	1,880

Chapter 4

Task 4.1

Answer 13,200	Units
Sales	13,800
Less: opening inventory (stock)	(2,100)
Add: closing inventory (stock)	1,500
Production	13,200

···

Task 4.2

Answer 189,500	Units
Sales	200,000
Less: opening inventory (stock)	(35,000)
Add: closing inventory (stock) (70% x 35,000)	24,500
Production	189,500

···

Task 4.3

Answer 7,500 units

Opening inventory (stock) + production (P) – closing inventory (stock) = sales

1,500 + P – 0 = 1.2 x P

1,500 = 0.2 P

P = 7,500

···

Task 4.4

Answer 16,702

Production required	=	16,200 x 100/97
	=	16,702 units

···

Task 4.5

	Period 1	Period 2	Period 3
Opening inventory (stock)	2,700	2,875	2,750
Production	10,975	11,375	11,050
Sales	10,800	11,500	11,000
Closing inventory (stock)	2,875	2,750	2,800

Working

	Period 1 Units	Period 2 Units	Period 3 Units
Sales	10,800	11,500	11,000
Less: opening inventory (stock)	(2,700)	(2,875)	(2,750)
Add: closing inventory (stock)			
11,500 x 25%	2,875		
11,000 x 25%		2,750	
11,200 x 25%			2,800
Production units required	10,975	11,375	11,050

Task 4.6

	Period 1	Period 2	Period 3
Required units	12,000	11,000	12,500
Manufactured units	12,500	11,459	13,021

Working for example for period 1

12,000 x 100/96 = 12,500

If the answer is not a round number it must be rounded up to ensure sufficient units are produced.

Task 4.7

Answer 141,112

Materials usage:	Kg
25,400 x 5 kgs	127,000
Add: wastage 127,000 x 10/90	14,112
Raw material required	141,112

Task 4.8

Materials usage budget

40,000 units x 5 kgs = 200,000 kgs

Materials purchases budget

	Kg
Raw materials required	200,000
Less: opening inventory (stock)	(30,000)
Add: closing inventory (stock)	
(30,000 x 80%)	24,000
	194,000

....

Task 4.9

	Period 1
Materials usage budget in kg	320,000
Materials purchases budget in kg	343,500
Materials purchases budget in £	858,750

Materials usage budget

	Period 1 Kg
Production 32,000 x 8 kgs	256,000
Normal loss 256,000 x 20/80	64,000
Materials usage	320,000

Materials purchasing budget – units

	Period 1 Kg
Materials usage	320,000
Less: opening inventory (stock)	(64,000)
Add: closing inventory (stock)	
35,000 x 8kg x 100/80 x 25%	87,500
	343,500

Materials purchasing budget – value

	Period 1 £
343,500 kg x £2.50	858,750

....

Task 4.10

Answer 400 hours

One unit requires	18 x 100/90	=	20 hours
20 units require	20 x 20	=	400 hours

Task 4.11

Answer 400,000

Standard hours	120,000 x 4	=	480,000 hours
Actual hours	480,000 x 100/120	=	400,000 hours

Task 4.12

Production budget

	Units
Sales	102,000
Less: opening inventory (stock)	(17,000)
Add: closing inventory (stock) (115,000 x 10/60)	19,167
Production	104,167

Labour usage budget

	Hours
Standard hours 104,167 x 5.5	572,919
Actual hours 572,919 x 100/95	603,073

Labour usage budget = 603,073 hours

Task 4.13

	Period 1
Sales budget (£)	
Production budget (units)	
Materials usage budget (kg)	
Materials purchasing budget (kg)	
Labour budget (hours)	
Labour budget (£)	

Working

	Period 1
	£
Sales budget (3,000 x £40)	120,000
Production budget	
	Units
Sales	3,000
Less: opening inventory (stock)	(600)
Add: closing inventory (stock)	
£3,400 x 20%	680
	3,080
Defective units	
£3,080 x 3/97 (rounded up)	96
	3,176
Materials usage budget	
	Kg
Production 3,176 x 4kg	12,704
Normal loss (x 10/90)	1,412
Materials usage	14,116
Materials purchasing budget	
	Kg
Materials usage	14,116
Less opening inventory (stock)	(4,200)
Add closing inventory (stock)	
16,040 x 35%	5,614
Purchases	15,530
Labour budget – hours	
	Hours
Standard hours	
Production 3,176 x 2	6,352
Idle time (hours x 20/80)	1,588
Total hours	7,940
Labour budget – £	
	£
7,940 x £8	63,520

Task 4.14

Production days   =   12 x 5   =   60 days

Closing inventory (stock) of finished goods:

Aye   =   1,500 x 5/60   =   125 units

Bee   =   2,400 x 5/60   =   200 units

Labour hours available before overtime

=   12 weeks x 35 hours x 70 employees

=   29,400 hours

Production budget

	Aye Units	Bee Units
Sales	1,500	2,400
Less opening inventory (stock)	(160)	(300)
Add closing inventory (stock)	125	200
	1,465	2,300
Faulty production		
1,465 x 2/98	30	
2,300 x 2.5/97.5		59
	1,495	2,359

Materials purchases

	Kg
1,495 x 4kg	5,980
2,359 x 7kg	16,513
Material usage	22,493
Less opening inventory (stock)	(2,800)
Add closing inventory (stock) (22,493 x 6/60)	2,250
Materials purchases	21,943

Materials purchases budget – 21,943 x £10   £219,430

Answer bank

Labour budget – hours

	Hours
Standard hours	
Aye 1,495 x 10 hours	14,950
Bee 2,359 x 7 hours	16,513
	31,463

Labour budget – value

	£
Standard rate: (35 x 12 x 70) = 29,400 hours x £8	235,200
Overtime: (31,463 – 29,400) = 2,063 hours x £8 x 1.5	24,756
	259,956

Cost savings:

	Opening inventory (stock)	Closing inventory (stock)	Reduction	Saving £
Aye	160	125	35 x £6 =	210
Bee	300	200	100 x £7 =	700
Raw materials	2,800	2,250	550 x £2 =	1,100
				2,010

....

Task 4.15

(i) Gross production budget

	Period 1 Units		Period 2 Units		Period 3 Units		Period 4 Units
Sales		19,400		21,340		23,280	22,31
Closing stock (W1)	4,268		4,656		4,462		4,462
Opening stock	3,880		4,268		4,656		4,462
Increase/(decrease) in							
stock		388		388		(194)	
Good production		19,788		21,728		23,086	22,31
Faulty production (W2)		612		672		714	69
Gross production		20,400		22,400		23,800	23,00

Workings

1 There are 20 days in each period.

Closing inventory (stock) = 4 days' sales in the next period = 4/20 of next period's sales

Closing inventory in period 1 = 4/20 x 21,340 =	4,268
Closing inventory in period 2 = 4/20 x 23,280=	4,656
Closing inventory in period 3 = 4/20 x 22,310 =	4,462
Closing inventory in period 4 = 4/20 x 22,310 =	4,462

2 3% of gross production is scrapped. Good production therefore represents 97% (or 97/100) of gross production. Faulty production is 3% (or 3/100) of gross production and hence 3/97 of good production.

Faulty production is 3/97 x good production.

(ii) **Material purchases budget**

	Period 1 Litres		Period 2 Litres		Period 3 Litres	
Material used in production (W1)		61,200		67,200		71,400
Closing inventory (W2)	16,800		17,850		17,250	
Opening inventory	16,500		16,800		17,850	
Increase/(decrease) in inventory		300		1,050		(600)
Purchases (litres)		61,500		68,250		70,800

Workings

1   Each unit requires three litres of material.

Material used in production = 3 × gross production (calculated in (i) above)

Material used in production, period 1 = 3 × 20,400 =   61,200
Material used in production, period 2 = 3 × 22,400 =   67,200
Material used in production, period 3 = 3 × 23,800 =   71,400

2   ▪   There are 20 days in each period.

▪   Closing inventory (stock) must equal five days' gross production in the next period.

▪   Each unit requires three litres of material.

▪   Closing inventory in period 1 = 5/20 × 22,400 (from (i) above) × 3 = 16,800

Closing inventory in period 2 = 5/20 × 23,800 × 3 = 17,850

Closing inventory in period 3 = 5/20 × 23,000 × 3 = 17,250

(iii) **Cost of material purchases**

	Period 1	Period 2	Period 3
Material to be purchased (from (ii))	61,500 litres	68,250 litres	70,800 litres
Cost per litre	× £8	× £8	× £8
Cost of material purchases	£492,000	£546,000	£566,400

(iv) **Labour budget**

	Period 1	Period 2	Period 3
Gross production (units) (from (i))	20,400	22,400	23,800
Labour hrs required per unit	× 0.5	× 0.5	× 0.5
Labour hrs required	10,200	11,200	11,900

(v) Cost of labour budget

Labour hrs required	10,200	11,200	11,900
Basic labour hrs available *	11,200	11,200	11,200
Surplus hrs/(overtime hrs)	1,000	–	(700)

* 70 workers × 40 hrs per wk × 4 wks = 11,200

	Period 1 £	Period 2 £	Period 3 £
Labour cost per period (guaranteed) *	67,200	67,200	67,200
Cost of overtime (700 × £9)	–	–	6,300
Cost of labour	67,200	67,200	73,500

* 70 workers x £240 x 4 wks

....

Task 4.16

	Quarter 1	Quarter 2	Quarter 3	Quarter 4
Surplus/(shortage) in current labour budget (hours)	2,880	1,380	(120)	(1,320)
Revised labour (hours)	9,360	12,180	12,180	12,180
Revised production (units)	3,120	4,060	4,060	4,060
Revised sales forecast (units)	3,000	3,300	4,000	4,300

Surplus/(shortage) in current labour budget

	Quarter 1	Quarter 2	Quarter 3	Quarter 4
Labour hours required	9,300	10,800	12,300	13,500
Guaranteed hours (W)	12,180	12,180	12,180	12,180
Surplus hours/(overtime hours)	2,880	1,380	(120)	(1,320)

Working

Guaranteed hours = 35 hours × 12 weeks × 29 workers

Revised budget of labour hours to reduce overtime

By rescheduling overtime as shown in the budget below, the total overtime hours can be reduced, with production being carried out within guaranteed hours in quarters 1 and 2, when there are surplus hours.

	Quarter 1	Quarter 2	Quarter 3	Quarter 4
Surplus hours/(overtime hours)	2,880	1,380	(120)	(1,320)
Original hours worked	9,300	10,800	12,300	13,500
Reschedule quarter 3's overtime		120	(120)	
Reschedule quarter 4's overtime	60	1,260		(1,320)
Revised labour hours	9,360	12,180	12,180	12,180

Revised production budget

A revised production budget which takes account of the rescheduling above is shown below.

	Quarter 1	Quarter 2	Quarter 3	Quarter 4
Revised labour hours (above)	9,360	12,180	12,180	12,180
Revised production budget (W)	3,120	4,060	4,060	4,060

Check: Total revised production = 15,300 units = original production (3,100 + 3,600 + 4,100 + 4,500)

Working

Labour hours per unit = 9,300 hours/3,100 units (from original budget) = 3 hours per unit.

Forecast trend

Using the regression line y = 1,000 + 100x established by the sales director, the trend for quarters 1 to 4 can be established (with x in quarter 1 = 25).

Quarter 1:	1,000 + (100 × 25) = 3,500 units
Quarter 2:	1,000 + (100 × 26) = 3,600 units
Quarter 3:	1,000 + (100 × 27) = 3,700 units
Quarter 4:	1,000 + (100 × 28) = 3,800 units

Forecast sales volume

The forecast sales volume is established by adjusting the trend values, set out above, by the seasonal variations, calculated by the sales director.

Quarter 1:	3,500 – 500 = 3,000 units
Quarter 2:	3,600 – 300 = 3,300 units
Quarter 3:	3,700 + 300 = 4,000 units
Quarter 4:	3,800 + 500 = 4,300 units

Chapter 5

Task 5.1

	October	November	December
Budgeted cash receipts from sales (£)	262,000	266,500	250,000

Workings		**October**	**November**	**December**
		£	**£**	**£**
Cash sales	280,000 x 30%	84,000		
	250,000 x 30%		75,000	
	220,000 x 30%			66,000
Credit sales				
August	240,000 x 30%	72,000		
September	265,000 x 40%	106,000		
	265,000 x 30%		79,500	
October	280,000 x 40%		112,000	
	280,000 x 30%			84,000
November	250,000 x 40%			100,000
Total cash receipts		262,000	266,500	250,000

Task 5.2

	October	November	December
Budgeted cash payments for purchases (£)	174,490	182,450	199,620

Workings

		October £	November £	December £
August	180,000 x 35%	63,000		
September	165,000 x 45%	74,250		
	165,000 x 35%		57,750	
October	190,000 x 20% x 98%	37,240		
	190,000 x 45%		85,500	
	190,000 x 35%			66,500
November	200,000 x 20% x 98%		39,200	
	200,000 x 45%			90,000
December	220,000 x 20% x 98%			43,120
Total cash payments		174,490	182,450	199,620

....

Task 5.3

	August	September	October
Budgeted cash payments to suppliers (£)	150,000	156,000	165,000

Workings

	August £	September £	October £
July purchases 5,000 x £50 x 60%	150,000		
August purchases 5,200 x £50 x 60%		156,000	
September purchases 5,500 x £50 x 60%			165,000

....

Task 5.4

Assume no opening and closing inventory (stock)

Forecast annual sales of £6,000 and a mark up of 33⅓%, means forecast purchases of £4,500

Forecast annual purchases of £12,000 and a margin of 20%, means forecast sales of £15,000

Forecast annual sales of £16,000 and forecast annual profits of £6,000, mean forecast mark-up of £60% and margin of £37½%

Working

Tutorial note. In this question you are told that there is no opening and closing inventory (stock), therefore purchases = cost of sales.

Remember **mark up** is on **purchases**.

If purchases 100%, mark up 33⅓,

Sales = 100 + 33⅓ = 133⅓%

$$\text{Purchases} = \frac{100}{133\frac{1}{3}} \times 6{,}000$$

$$= £4{,}500$$

Remember **margin** is on **sales**.

If sales 100% margin 20%

Purchases = 100 − 20 = 80%

$$\text{Sales} = \frac{100}{80} \times 12{,}000$$

$$= £15{,}000$$

$$\text{Mark up} = \frac{\text{Profits}}{\text{Purchases}}$$

$$= \frac{6{,}000}{16{,}000 - 6{,}000}$$

$$= 60\%$$

$$\text{Margin} = \frac{\text{Profits}}{\text{Sales}}$$

$$= \frac{6{,}000}{16{,}000}$$

$$= 37\frac{1}{2}\%$$

Task 5.5

	April	May	June
Budgeted cash receipts for sales (£)	600,500	560,650	539,375

		April	May	June
		£	£	£
March sales	650,000 x 70%	455,000		
April sales	600,000 x 25% x 97%	145,500		
	600,000 x 70%		420,000	
May sales	580,000 x 25% x 97%		140,650	
	580,000 x 70%			406,000
June sales	550,000 x 25% x 97%	_____	_____	133,375
Total cash receipts		600,500	560,650	539,375

. . . .

Task 5.6

	April	May	June
Budgeted cash wages payments (£)	19,740	18,060	16,800

Production budget

	March	April	May	June
	Units	Units	Units	Units
Sales next month	7,200	7,050	6,550	6,150
Less: opening inventory (stock)	(1,000)	(1,000)	(1,000)	(900)
Add: closing inventory (stock)	1,000	1,000	900	750
Production in units	7,200	7,050	6,450	6,000

Labour budget hours

	April	May	June
	Hours	Hours	Hours
7,050/3	2,350		
6,450/3		2,150	
6,000/3			2,000

Labour budget – £

	April	May	June
	£	£	£
Hours x £8.40	19,740	18,060	16,800

Task 5.7

Cash budget – July to September

	July	August	September
	£	£	£
Cash receipts:			
Sales (W1)	438,400	467,840	488,520
Proceeds from sale of equipment	——	7,500	——
Total receipts	438,400	475,340	488,520
Cash payments:			
Purchases (W2)	246,000	256,000	288,000
Wages	60,000	60,000	60,000
Overheads (W3)	44,000	47,750	49,000
Selling expenses	48,000	50,000	52,000
Equipment		42,000	
Overdraft interest	820	424	233
Total payments	398,820	456,174	449,233
Net cash flow for the month	39,580	19,166	39,287
Opening balance	(82,000)	(42,420)	(23,254)
Closing balance	(42,420)	(23,254)	16,033

WORKINGS

(1) **Receipts from credit sales**

		July	August	September
		£	£	£
April sales	420,000 x 12%	50,400		
May sales	400,000 x 25%	100,000		
	400,000 x 12%		48,000	
June sales	480,000 x 40%	192,000		
	480,000 x 25%		120,000	
	480,000 x 12%			57,600
July sales	500,000 x 20% x 96%	96,000		
	500,000 x 40%		200,000	
	500,000 x 25%			125,000
August sales	520,000 x 20% x 96%		99,840	
	520,000 x 40%			208,000
September sales	510,000 x 20% x 96%			97,920
		438,400	467,840	488,520

(2) **Payments to suppliers**

		July	August	September
		£	£	£
May purchases	250,000 x 60%	150,000		
June purchases	240,000 x 40%	96,000		
	240,000 x 60%		144,000	
July purchases	280,000 x 40%		112,000	
	280,000 x 60%			168,000
August purchases	300,000 x 40%			120,000
		246,000	256,000	288,000

(3) **Overheads**

		July	August	September
		£	£	£
June overheads	(50,000 – 6,000) x 25%	11,000		
July overheads	(50,000 – 6,000) x 75%	33,000		
	(50,000 – 6,000) x 25%		11,000	
August overheads				
	(55,000 – 6,000) x 75%		36,750	
	(55,000 – 6,000) x 25%			12,250
September overheads				
	(55,000 – 6,000) x 75%			36,750
		44,000	47,750	49,000

··

Task 5.8

Tutorial note. Don't get caught out by putting all the rent in the budget.

Cash budget: July to September

	July	August	September
	£000	£000	£000
Inflows			
Sales	160	320	80
Outflows			
Purchases	60	40	120
Salaries	36	36	36
Rent (£48,000 ÷ 4)	12	—	—
Total payments	108	76	156
Net cash flow for month	52	244	(76)
Opening balance	(112)	(60)	184
Closing balance	(60)	184	108

··

Task 5.9

Cash budget – October to December

	October	November	December
	£	£	£
Cash receipts:			
Sales (W1)	378,000	391,500	417,000
Cash payments:			
Purchases of raw materials (W2)	144,180	156,060	164,880
Wages (W3)	118,800	127,440	131,760
Production overheads	50,000	50,000	50,000
General overheads	60,000	60,000	68,000
Total payments	372,980	393,500	414,640
Net cash flow for the month	5,020	(2,000)	2,360
Opening balance	40,000	45,020	43,020
Closing balance	45,020	43,020	45,380

Workings

(1) **Receipts from credit sales**

	October	November	December
	£	£	£
August sales			
5,000 x £75 x 60%	225,000		
September sales			
5,100 x £75 x 40%	153,000		
5,100 x £75 x 60%		229,500	
October sales			
5,400 x £75 x 40%		162,000	
5,400 x £75 x 60%			243,000
November sales			
5,800 x £75 x 40%			174,000
	378,000	391,500	417,000

(2) **Purchases of raw materials**

Production budget

	Aug	Sept	Oct	Nov	Dec
	Units	Units	Units	Units	Units
Sales	5,000	5,100	5,400	5,800	6,000
Less: opening inventory (stock)	(500)	(500)	(500)	(600)	(700)
Add: closing inventory (stock)	500	500	600	700	800
Production	5,000	5,100	5,500	5,900	6,100

Purchases budget

	Aug	Sept	Oct	Nov
	Kg	Kg	Kg	Kg
Required for next month's production x 3kg	15,300	16,500	17,700	18,300
Less: opening inventory (stock)	(3,000)	(3,000)	(3,000)	(3,200)
Add: closing inventory (stock)	3,000	3,000	3,200	3,500
Purchases in kg	15,300	16,500	17,900	18,600
	£	£	£	£
Kg x £9	137,700	148,500	161,100	167,400

Payments to suppliers

	October	November	December
	£	£	£
August purchases			
137,700 x 40%	55,080		
September purchases			
148,500 x 60%	89,100		
148,500 x 40%		59,400	
October purchases			
161,100 x 60%		96,660	
161,100 x 40%			64,440
November purchases			
167,400 x 60%			100,440
Total payments to suppliers	144,180	156,060	164,880

(3) **Wages**

Labour budget – hours

	Oct	Nov	Dec
Production units (W2)	5,500	5,900	6,100
x 3 hours = labour usage (hours)	16,500	17,700	18,300
	£	£	£
Wages – production x £7.20	118,800	127,440	131,760

Task 5.10

Cash inflows from sales = opening receivables (debtors) + sales – closing receivables

= £23,000 + £228,400 - £19,000

= £232,400

Cash outflows on purchases = opening payables (creditors) + purchases – closing payables

= £5,600 +£128,000 - £12,800 = £120,800

Chapter 6

Task 6.1

Answer: Machine hours

The business can sell 12,000 units

The business has enough material to make 25,000/2 = 12,500 units

The business has enough machine hours (5 x 1,000 = 5,000 hours) to make 5,000/0.5 = 10,000 units

The business has enough labour hours (40 x 500 = 20,000 hours) to make 20,000/1.5 = 13,333 units

Therefore, the machine hours limit production to 10,000 units despite the sales demand being greater than this.

Task 6.2

Total production	=	$\dfrac{129{,}000\,\text{kgs}}{5\,\text{kgs}}$
	=	25,800 units
Monthly production	=	$\dfrac{25{,}800\,\text{kgs}}{12}$
	=	2,150 units

Task 6.3

Maximum shortage

	July	Aug	Sept	Oct	Nov	Dec
Requirement	4,800	4,300	4,100	4,900	4,200	5,000
Purchase	4,500	4,300	4,100	4,500	4,200	4,500
Shortfall	300	–	–	400	–	500

Total shortfall	=	300 + 400 + 500
	=	1,200 units

Purchasing plan

	July	Aug	Sept	Oct	Nov	Dec
Requirement	4,800	4,300	4,100	4,900	4,200	5,000
Purchase	4,500	4,500	4,500	4,500	4,500	4,500
Excess/(Shortfall)	(300)	200	400	(400)	300	(500)
Inventory (stock)	–	200	600	200	500	–
Production	4,500	4,300	4,100	4,900	4,200	5,000

By purchasing the maximum available in August, September and November, even though it is not required, the shortages in October and December can be covered from materials held in inventory (stock). This leaves only the 300 kg shortage in July.

....

Task 6.4

(a) If the shortage is only temporary then there are a number of short-term solutions which could alleviate the problem.

- Using inventory (stock) of materials – the inventory (stock) of raw materials could be run down in order to maintain production and sales.

- Using inventory (stock) of finished goods – in order to maintain sales in the short-term, finished goods inventory (stock) can be run down even though production levels are not as high as would be liked.

- Rescheduling purchases – if the amount of the raw material required is available in some periods but not in others, then the raw materials purchases could be rescheduled to ensure that the maximum use is made of the available materials.

(b) If the shortage is a long-term problem then the following are possible options for the business.

- Seeking an alternative supplier – this is an obvious solution but it may not always be possible to find another supplier who can supply the correct quality at an acceptable price.

- Finding an alternative material – in some instances a product can only be made from one particular material but it may be possible to adapt the design of the product and the manufacturing process in order to use a substitute material that is widely available.

- Manufacturing an alternative product – it may be possible to switch the production process to manufacture an alternative product which uses a different material which is not in short supply.

- Buying in finished goods for resale – instead of producing the product, it could be purchased in finished form from another producer who is not having the same problems with supply of the materials required. However this probably would lead to an under-utilisation of production resources and a major change in the organisation's strategy.

....

Task 6.5

	May	June	July	Aug	Sept	Oct
Material requirement	9,500	10,200	10,200	9,300	10,200	10,300
Potential shortage	–	200	200	–	200	300

Do not buy 10,000 kgs each month as this will lead to inventory (stock) that is not required. However buy enough in May and August to cover the potential shortages.

	May	June	July	Aug	Sept	Oct
Material requirement	9,500	10,200	10,200	9,300	10,200	10,300
Purchases	9,900	10,000	10,000	9,800	10,000	10,000
Inventory (stock)	400	200	–	500	300	–
Production	9,500	10,200	10,200	9,300	10,200	10,300

No shortage

Task 6.6

Total hours available (including overtime)	=	12 x (38 + 8)
	=	552 hours per week
Maximum production	=	552/3
	=	184 units

Possible solutions to this problem could be:

- increase the overtime worked – it may be possible to agree additional overtime with the employees in order to maintain production; however at 46 hours per week already, this may not be an option here

- use sub-contractors – in some types of business it may be possible to use agency workers or to sub-contract the work in order to maintain production levels. This option is likely to be fairly costly

- use up finished goods inventory (stock) – if production levels are lower than required to meet sales demand, then for the short term sales can still be maintained by running down the finished goods inventory (stock). This is not, however, a long-term solution

- buying in finished goods inventory (stock) – this could be an expensive option leaving factory capacity under-utilised and may have quality implications as well

- improving labour efficiency – this is not something that can be done quickly but with training over a period of time it may be possible to increase the number of employees with the skills required

Task 6.7

Labour hours required	=	1,860 units x 4 hours
	=	7,440 hours
Labour hours available	=	160 employees x 35 hours
	=	5,600 hours
Overtime hours required	=	7,440 – 5,600
	=	1,840 hours

Task 6.8

Hours of production line time	=	2 shifts x 7 hours x 5 days x 2 production lines
	=	140 hours
Maximum production	=	140 hours x 30 units
	=	4,200 units

If sales demand exceeds this maximum production level there are a number of options that could be considered.

- introduce a third shift so that the production lines are in fact running for 21 hours a day.

- lengthen the shift to, say, a 9 hour shift.

- operate the factory for 6 or even 7 days a week.

- speed up the production line so that more units are produced an hour.

Task 6.9

Any three of the following:

- limitations on the amount of raw materials that can be purchased

- manpower limitations – a limit to the number of hours that can be worked in the period by the labour force

- capacity limitations – a limit to the number of machine hours available

- a limit to the quantity that can be produced by a production line in the period

Task 6.10

There would appear to be no limits regarding demand for beds or the labour force. The key budget factor would seem to be the number of beds available.

In a busy shopping centre demand for the ice cream is probably not the key factor therefore it is likely to be the quantity of ice cream that can be stored each day.

Sales demand is not a limiting factor however as this is highly skilled work the available hours of the three partners will be the key budget factor.

As the products are similar to those of other manufacturers and therefore can be replaced by similar products by the retail stores then it is highly likely that the demand from the retail stores will be the key budget factor.

Task 6.11

	Production units
Product W	300
Product X	250
Product Y	0
Product Z	1,000

Workings

	W (£)	X (£)	Y (£)	Z (£)
Sales price	200	90	180	150
Materials cost	(60)	(24)	(57)	(36)
Labour (hours)	(24)	(30)	(72)	(36)
Contribution	116	36	51	78

Kg/unit	20	8	19	12
Contribution/kg	£5.80	£4.50	£2.68	£6.50
Rank	2	3	4	1
Production	300	250	0	1,000
Kg used in production	6,000	2,000	0	12,000

Chapter 7

Task 7.1

Answer £20,000

£15,000 is the cost of 3 supervisors therefore each one costs £5,000 per period.

At a production level of 330,000 units four production supervisors will be required costing £20,000 for the period.

Task 7.2

	112,000 units
	£
Materials (112,000 x £2.40) (W)	268,800
Labour (112,000 x £1) + 24,000 (W)	136,000
Production overhead (fixed)	38,000

Working

Materials	100,000 units	£2.40 per unit
	120,000 units	£2.40 per unit

Therefore a variable cost – £2.40 per unit

Labour	100,000 units	£1.24 per unit
	120,000 units	£1.20 per unit

Therefore a semi-variable cost

Variable element	=	£20,000/20,000 units
	=	£1 per unit

At 100,000 units:	£
Variable cost	100,000
Fixed cost (bal fig)	24,000
Total cost	124,000

Task 7.3

Production overhead (72,000 x £7) + £104,000 (W) = £608,000

Working

$$\text{Variable element of cost} = \frac{£664,000 - 524,000}{20,000 \text{ units}}$$

$$= £7 \text{ per unit}$$

At 60,000 units:	£
Variable element 60,000 x £7	420,000
Fixed element (bal fig)	104,000
Total cost	524,000

Answer bank

Task 7.4

	Budget	Flexed budget
	20,000 units	**15,000 units**
	£	**£**
Sales	130,000	97,500
Material	(55,000)	(41,250)
Labour (8 x £3,500)	(35,000)	(28,000)
Production overhead	(18,000)	(18,000)
Gross profit	22,000	10,250
General expenses (6,400 + 15,000 x £0.28)	12,000	10,600
Operating profit/(loss)	10,000	(350)

Task 7.5

	Budget	Actual	Variances
	28,000 units	**31,500 units**	
	£	**£**	**£**
Sales	406,000	441,000	35,000 (F)
Materials	165,200	180,400	15,200 (A)
Labour	100,800	115,600	14,800 (A)
Production overhead	37,500	39,000	1,500 (A)
Gross profit	102,500	106,000	3,500 (F)
General expenses	55,600	68,900	13,300 (A)
Operating profit	46,900	37,100	9,800 (A)

	Flexed budget	Actual	Variances
	31,500 units	31,500 units	
	£	£	£
Sales	456,750	441,000	15,750 (A)
Materials	185,850	180,400	5,450 (F)
Labour	113,400	115,600	2,200 (A)
Production overhead	37,500	39,000	1,500 (A)
Gross profit	120,000	106,000	14,000 (A)
General expenses (W)	60,850	68,900	8,050 (A)
Operating profit	59,150	37,100	22,050 (A)

Working

General expenses:

At 28,000 units – Variable element = £55,600 – 13,600/28,000
                                      = £1.50 per unit

	£
At 31,500 units:	
Variable element 31,500 x £1.50	47,250
Fixed element	13,600
Total cost	60,850

Reason for difference in variances

The variances calculated when using the original fixed budget show favourable sales and gross profit variances and fairly large adverse cost variances culminating in an adverse net profit variance. However this is not comparing like with like since the original budget is for 28,000 units whereas the actual activity level is greater at 31,500 and therefore, in view of the higher activity level, both costs and revenues would be expected to be higher than originally budgeted.

When the actual results are compared to the flexed budget the variances are different. These variances reflect a truer picture since we are now comparing the actual costs and revenue for 31,500 units with a budget adjusted for the same level of activity.

There is an adverse sales variance and an adverse gross profit variance. The materials now show a favourable variance and the other variances are not so large. The final net profit variance however is much larger than the variance when compared to the fixed budget.

Task 7.6

	Flexed budget		Actual		Variances
	230,000 units		230,000 units		
	£	£	£	£	£
Sales		1,564,000		1,532,000	32,000 (A)
Materials	793,500		783,200		10,300 (F)
Labour	433,500		428,600		4,900 (F)
Production expenses	180,000		173,500		6,500 (F)
Production cost		1,407,000		1,385,300	
Gross profit		157,000		146,700	10,300 (A)
General expenses		72,000		74,700	2,700 (A)
Operating profit		85,000		72,000	13,000 (A)

Working

Sales – variable = £1,360,000/200,000 = £1,632,000/240,000 = £6.80 per unit

Materials – variable cost = £690,000/200,000 = £828,000/240,000 = £3.45 per unit

Labour – semi-variable cost

Variable element	=	$\dfrac{£449,000 - 387,000}{40,000}$
	=	£1.55
Fixed element	=	£387,000 – (200,000 x 1.55)
	=	£77,000
At 230,000	=	£77,000 + (230,000 x 1.55)
	=	£433,500

Production expenses – semi-variable cost

Variable element	=	$\dfrac{£186,000 - 162,000}{40,000}$
	=	£0.60 per unit
Fixed element	=	£162,000 – (200,000 x 0.60)
	=	£42,000
At 230,000	=	£42,000 + (230,000 x 0.60)
	=	£180,000

Task 7.7

Quarter 2 budget

	£	£
Sales 50,000 units		400,000
Materials	165,400	
Labour	69,800	
Cost of production: 56,000 units @ £4.20	235,200	
Less: closing inventory (stock)	25,200	
Cost of sales		210,000
Contribution		190,000
Production overhead		56,000
General expenses		52,000
Operating profit		82,000

	£
Profit per absorption costing budget	88,000
Less: production overhead included in closing inventory (stock) (6,000 x £1)	(6,000)
Profit per marginal costing budget	82,000

Task 7.8

The marketing or sales overhead variance may be favourable if the sales director is not immediately replaced, as the cost of the salary of the director is not incurred. However, if costs of recruitment are incurred, there may be an adverse administration or HR overhead variance.

There will be no effect on the sales variance, even if the volume sold decreases as the variance will be calculated after the budget has been flexed to actual activity levels.

Task 7.9

An adverse administrative overheads variance may be reported. This is because the administrative overheads will have increased as the salary of the credit controller would still have been paid while the external agency was also paid. The adverse variance may also be increased by the increase in irrecoverable (bad) debts if there was a break between the credit controller taking sick leave and the external agency being appointed.

Task 7.10

The importance of identifying controllable variances is in the area of motivation or de-motivation of management. If variances are reported, as part of the responsibility of a manager, over which he has no control, then this will have a de-motivational effect. If a manager is constantly held responsible for an adverse variance in a cost, the level of which he cannot influence, then this will not have a positive effect on the performance of this manager.

Investigating the causes of variances and determining any interdependence between the variances is an important aspect of management control because in a system of responsibility accounting the managers responsible for various elements of the business will be held accountable for the relevant variances. However they should only be held accountable for variances that are within their control.

There may be variances caused by factors which are beyond the manager's control, such as an increase in rent or business rates. There may also be variances in a manager's responsibility centre which have not been caused by his actions but by those of another responsibility centre manager.

An example is a favourable material price variance caused by purchasing a lower grade of material which leads directly to an adverse materials usage variance, as the lower grade of material means that there is greater wastage. The initial reaction might be to give credit to the purchasing manager for the favourable variance and to lay blame for the adverse usage variance on the production manager. However the true picture is that, in the absence of any further reasons for the variance then the responsibility for both variances lies with the purchasing manager.

Task 7.11

The process of continual comparison of actual results to budgeted results is known as feedback.

The budget period is normally for the forthcoming year; however, the feedback process should take place on a much more frequent basis. The calculation and reporting of variances should take place on a regular basis and will be daily, weekly or monthly depending upon the organisation. Any resulting action that must be taken in order to eliminate variances or improve efficiency should then be taken as soon as possible.

The information that is being received about the current performance of the business in terms of the current actual results can then also be used to influence the budget for future periods. This system of using information about the current performance for budgeting for the future is known as feedforward.

Task 7.12

Units	Flexed budget 34,000		Actual 34,000		Variance
	£	£	£	£	£
Sales (34,000 x £22) (W)		748,000		697,000	51,000 (A)
Direct costs					
Materials (34,000 x £8.40) (W)	285,600		299,200		13,600 (A)
Factory power					
(34,000 x £2.10) (W)	71,400		68,000		3,400 (F)
		357,000		367,200	
Contribution		391,000		329,800	
Labour	180,000		192,600		12,600 (A)
Factory power	20,600		20,600		–
Fixed overheads	75,000		79,000		4,000 (A)
Fixed costs		275,600		292,200	
Operating profit		115,400		37,600	77,800 (A)

Workings

Budgeted unit selling price	=	$\frac{£660,000}{30,000}$
	=	£22 per unit
Budgeted unit material cost	=	$\frac{£252,000}{30,000}$
	=	£8.40 per unit
Marginal element of factory power	=	£83,600 – £20,600
	=	£63,000
Budgeted marginal cost per unit	=	$\frac{£63,000}{30,000}$
	=	£2.10 per unit
Actual marginal cost	=	£88,600 – £20,600
	=	£68,000

Explanation of why the flexed budget operating statement shows different results from that of the original budget

The original budget was a fixed budget based upon the budgeted sales and production of 30,000 units. The flexed budget is based upon sales and production of 34,000 units therefore the anticipated increases in sales revenue and variable costs is built into this budget.

Task 7.13

Flexible budget comparison

	Flexed budget	Actual	Variance £
Production and sales units	22,000 units	22,000 units	
	£	£	
Variable costs:			
Material (22,000 x £9)	198,000	214,320	16,320 (A)
Labour (22,000 x £12)	264,000	255,200	8,800 (F)
Semi-variable costs			
Heat, light, power – variable (22,000 x £1) Fixed element £7,000	29,000	25,880	3,120 (F)
Fixed costs:			
Rent, rates, depreciation	40,000	38,000	2,000 (F)
Total costs	531,000	533,400	2,400 (A)

Workings

	Original budget	Revised budget	Difference	Variable cost per unit
Production and sales units	24,000	20,000	4,000	
	£	£	£	£
Variable costs				
Material	216,000	180,000	36,000 (÷ 4,000)	9
Labour	288,000	240,000	48,000 (÷ 4,000)	12
Semi-variable costs				
Heat, light and power	31,000	27,000	4,000 (÷ 4,000)	1

Calculation of fixed costs and variable unit costs

The fixed element of heat, light and power costs can now be determined using figures from the original budget.

	£
Total costs	31,000
Variable cost (24,000 units x £1)	24,000
Therefore fixed costs of heat, light and power	7,000

Actual costs revised for miscoded invoice: Material = £206,800 + £7,520 = £214,320

Heat, light etc = £33,400 - £7,520 = £25,880

Two reasons why a favourable cost variance may have arisen

(1) **Managers may have included unrealistically high costs in the original budget.** This is a problem which can arise with participative budgeting; managers include extra cost allowances to ensure that they achieve their budgets. The submitted budgets therefore need careful checking, although this may be difficult because the managers themselves are the ones with the technical expertise.

(2) **Costs may have been lower than the level expected when the original budget was determined.** For example, an expected rise in rent or rates costs may not have occurred. Such savings are not necessarily the result of management control action.

Two reasons why higher sales volume may not be the result of improved motivation

(1) The **market** for units may have **expanded** and the business could have reaped the benefit of a general increase in the demand for this product. This general market increase is not necessarily the result of improved motivation of sales staff.

(2) The sales staff may have **submitted an unrealistically low sales target** for the budget, to ensure that they achieve the target. Thus the fact that the sales volume is higher than budget may be a result of participative budgeting, but it may be due to manipulation of the system rather than improved motivation.

Task 7.14

Flexed budget statement

	Flexed budget	Actual results	Variances
Production and sales volume (CD players)	140,000	140,000	
	£'000	£'000	£'000
Conversion costs			
Labour (W1)	1,000	972	28 (F)
Light, heat and power (W2)	610	586	24 (F)
Rent, rates and insurance (W3)	200	200	–
Depreciation (W4)	150	132	18 (F)
Total conversion costs	1,960	1,890	70 (F)
Bought-in materials (W5)	2,800	3,220	420 (A)
Total expenses	4,760	5,110	350 (A)
Revenue (turnover) (W6)	5,600	6,440	840 (F)
Operating profit	840	1,330	490 (F)

Workings

Budgeted selling price per CD player = revenue/sales volume

(£3,200,000/80,000 or £4,000,000/100,000) £40.00

Budgeted bought-in material cost per CD player = bought-in materials/ production volume (£1,600,000/80,000 or £2,000,000/100,000) £20.00

Labour unit variable cost

Using the incremental approach:

	Volume		Cost
	100,000		£760,000
	80,000		£640,000
Incremental volume of	20,000	has an incremental cost of	£120,000

Therefore variable cost per unit = £120,000/20,000 = £6 per unit

Budgeted total labour fixed cost

	£
Total cost	760,000
Total variable cost (£6 × 100,000)	600,000
Fixed cost	160,000

An identical answer is possible by using the total cost for 80,000 CD players and deducting the total variable cost based on 80,000 CD players.

Budgeted variable cost of light, heat and power

Using the incremental approach:

	Volume		Cost
	100,000		£450,000
	80,000		£370,000
Incremental volume of	20,000	has an incremental cost of	£80,000

Therefore variable cost per unit = £80,000/20,000 = £4 per unit

Budgeted total light, heat and power fixed cost

	£
Total cost	450,000
Total variable cost (£4 x 100,000)	400,000
Fixed cost	50,000

An identical answer is possible by using the total cost for 80,000 CD players and deducting the total variable cost based on 80,000 CD players.

Workings for flexed budget

1. Variable cost of 140,000 CD players + labour fixed cost = (£6 × 140,000) + £160,000 = £1,000,000

2. Variable cost of 140,000 CD players + light, heat and power fixed cost = (£4 × 140,000) + £50,000 = £610,000

3. Fixed cost so the same at all levels of production

4. Fixed cost so the same at all levels of production

5. Cost of 140,000 CD players = £20 × 140,000 = £2,800,000

6. Revenue (turnover) from 140,000 CD players = £40 × 140,000 = £5,600,000

MEMO

To: Chief Executive
From: Assistant management accountant
Date: xx.xx.xx
Subject: **Performance related pay**

Possible reasons for improved profit

The improved profitability may have occurred even without the introduction of performance related pay.

(1) The company cannot control the volume of sales as the only customer is the parent company. It therefore depends entirely on the level of demand from the parent company. This year they required 40,000 more CD players than budgeted and so, even without performance related pay, the sales volume target would have been exceeded. All other things being equal (ie no increase in fixed costs and variable costs per unit), this increase in demand would have increased profit.

(2) Part of the improved profit arose from an apparent change in accounting policy on depreciation. There were no non-current (fixed) asset purchases or sales and hence the actual annual depreciation figure would have been known and should have been the same as the budgeted figure. The actual figure was less than the budgeted figure and so actual profit was greater than budgeted.

(3) The selling price per CD player is set at twice the cost of the bought-in materials. This means the more managers pay for the bought-in materials, the higher the price they can charge the parent company and so the higher the profit we can report. (Such a policy leads to inefficiencies, however, as managers are motivated to pay as much as possible for bought-in materials.)

(4) Fixed costs are the same irrespective of the level of production and sales. Hence the contribution will increase, all other things being equal, if actual volumes are greater than budgeted volumes and, with fixed costs remaining constant, so will profitability.

Note: You were required to provide only three reasons.

General conditions for improved performance

There are several conditions necessary if performance related pay is to lead to improved performance.

(1) Managers need to know the objectives of the organisation.

(2) Budgets must tie in with those objectives.

(3) Managers must feel that the objectives are achievable (although they should provide a challenge).

(4) Managers must want to achieve those objectives.

(5) Managers must be able to influence the achievement of the objectives.

(6) The level of rewards – both financial and non-financial – should motivate managers.

(7) Managers must have the skills necessary to achieve the targets.

(8) There should be a short period of time between effort and reward.

(9) The actual results should not be capable of being manipulated.

Note: You were required to provide only three reasons.

Chapter 8

Task 8.1

Number of:

- website hits per day
- purchases per day
- purchases per hit
- customer accounts
- returns per order

....

Task 8.2

- a vet's surgery   –   animals seen per day
- a bar   –   drinks served per employee
- a firm of solicitors   –   chargeable hours as a percentage of total hours
- a retail store   –   sales per employee
                           –   sales per square metre of shop floor
- a wedding cake business –   number of cakes made per day
                           –   number of cakes decorated per day

....

Task 8.3

- Weight of shavings collected per day
- Cost of shavings collected per day.
- Weight of shavings collected per machine.
- Cost of storage of shavings before collection for scrap.
- Frequency/cost of rubbish collection service

....

Task 8.4

- Chargeable time of a trainee as a percentage of time spent in the office
- Cost of non-chargeable hours (because of training or lack of chargeable time in office)
- Cost of training per trainee
- Average time from joining firm to exam completion

....

Task 8.5

- Units produced per machine hour

- Total maintenance costs, and maintenance costs per machine

- Breakdowns (and so idle hours) per machine, or total lost machine hours per week/month

- Number of machines in operation per shift

Task 8.6

- Complaints per number of covers

- Time between order and meals being served

Task 8.7

Driver productivity

A possible measure of driver productivity is the number of miles per driver, or the number of journeys undertaken per driver.

Satisfaction of passenger needs indicators, using the information collected

The satisfaction of passenger needs could be monitored by the number of passengers per journey.

Depending on the size of the buses, passenger needs may be less satisfied if there are more passengers per journey because of more crowding or the need to stand because no seats were available.

Another measure of the satisfaction of passenger needs is the number of journeys per day, as this may mean reduced waiting times.

Satisfaction of passenger needs indicators, which would require other information

A measure of the satisfaction of customer needs that cannot be derived from the existing data is cleanliness of the buses.

Monitoring the cleaning cost per day or per bus might give some indication of the effort put into keeping the buses clean.

Another measure of the satisfaction of customer needs **is punctuality** of the buses and their **adherence to published** timetables.

Monitoring the percentage of buses arriving and departing within five minutes of their published time would give an indication of performance in this area.

Safety indicators, using existing information

The safety aspect of Travel Bus's operations could be monitored by the maintenance cost per mile, although a high cost may in fact indicate an older fleet, and so reduced safety.

Safety indicators, requiring other information

A measure of the safety aspect that cannot be derived from the existing data is the number of accidents per year.

Another measure could be the percentage of maintenance cost that is incurred to prevent faults compared with the percentage incurred to correct faults. This would indicate whether faults were being prevented before they occurred, or whether maintenance was being carried out 'after the event', which could compromise safety.

▪▪

Answer bank

SAMPLE ASSESSMENT 1
BUDGETING

Time allowed: 2 hours 30 minutes

Section 1

Task 1.1A

Match the data in the first column with the appropriate source in the second column.

Data	Source
Inflation trends in UK	Market Research
Value Added Tax (VAT) rates	Office for National Statistics
Demand for our products	SWOT analysis
	HMRC publications (Her Majesty's Customs & Revenue)
	Gross National Product
	New York Times

Task 1.1B

Whom would you contact in each of the following situations?

- You want to identify the production capacity of the firm. PROD. MAN
- You want to forecast the price of raw materials. BUYER
- The draft budget is ready for review. BUD. COM.

Choose from:

- Trade union representative
- Managing director
- Buyer
- Budget committee
- Production planning manager

Task 1.1C

Take each item of cost in the list below and place it into its appropriate budget.

Cost
Production wages
Printing recruitment application forms
Advertising
Customer demand survey
Raw material usage
Spare parts for production machines
Warehouse extension
Commission paid to sales staff

Personnel
APP. FORMS

Cost of production
PROD. WAGES
MAT USAGE

Maintenance
SPARE PARTS

Capital expenditure

WAREHOUSE

Marketing

ADVERT

CUST. DEMAND

COMM. TO SALES

Task 1.1D

Select an appropriate accounting treatment for each of the following costs:

- Holiday pay for production workers PROD. LAB/HR
- Material wastage in the production process DIRECT
- Cost of the purchasing department ACTIVITY BASED
- Administrative wages ADMIN
- Computing services ADMIN
- Production equipment maintenance LAB M/C HOUR
- Depreciation of production equipment LAB M/C HOUR
- Redecoration of the sales showroom MARK

Options available are:

- Allocate to marketing overheads
- Allocate to administrative overheads
- Direct cost
- Charge to production in a machine hour overhead rate
- Charge to production in a labour hour overhead rate
- Activity based charge to production cost centres

Task 1.1E

Calculate the appropriate budgeted overhead recovery rate for the following production department. The department's annual budget for indirect costs is:

	£
Indirect labour	17,000
Supervisor wages	19,000
Depreciation of equipment	4,000
Machine maintenance	3,500
Canteen subsidy	6,500
Total	**50,000**

Notes: The budget production of 2,500 units will require 5,000 machine hours and 25,000 direct labour hours.

Complete the following:

Overhead recovery should be based on **Labour hours** / ~~**Machine hours**~~ / ~~**Units produced**~~.

The recovery rate will be £ 2 per LAB HOUR

. . . .

Task 1.2A

Complete the following production forecast for product P.

Units of product P

	Week 1	Week 2	Week 3	Week 4	Week 5
Opening inventory (stock)	1,200	1500	1350	1650	2100
Production		6300	4850	4800	5950
Sub-total		7500	6350	6150	7600
Sales	6,000	5,000	4,500	5,500	7,000
Closing inventory (stock)		1500	1350	1650	2100

Closing inventory (stock) should be 30% of the following week's forecast sales.

. . . .

Task 1.2B

The quarterly production requirements for product L are shown below.

10% of production fails the quality checks and must be scrapped.

How many items of product L must be manufactured to allow for waste?

	Month 1	Month 2	Month 3
Required units	72,000	90,000	81,000
Manufactured units	80,000	100,000	90,000

Task 1.2C

Raw Material purchases

- 15,000 items of product M are to be manufactured in April.
- Each requires 1.5 metres of raw material.
- 10% of raw material is wasted during manufacture.
- The opening inventory (stock) will be 12,000 metres.
- The closing inventory (stock) will be 10,000 metres.

How much material must be purchased?

Select from:

- 9,111m
- 13,111mm
- 22,750m
- 23,000m
- 27,000m

Task 1.2D

Labour hours

- 36,000 units of product L are to be manufactured in May.
- Each one takes 5 minutes to produce.
- 15 staff will each work 180 hours basic time.

3000 HRS

2700 HRS = 300

How many overtime hours must be worked to complete the production?

Select from:

- 180
- 300
- 360
- 3,000
- 7,200

....

Task 1.2E

Department X manufactures three products, A, B and C.

Calculate the machine hours required to manufacture these in November.

Product	Units	Hours per unit	Hours required
A	140	1.5	210
B	210	2.0	420
C	170	3.0	510
Total hours for department X			1140

There are three machines in the department.

Each machine can be used for 250 hours in November. Additional machines can be hired if required.

How many additional machines should be hired?

2

....

Task 1.2F

You are required to complete the workings schedules and Operating Budget below.

Workings schedules			Operating budget	Units	£
Materials	**kg**	**£**	Sales revenue @ £2.60 each	29,000	75.400
Opening inventory (stock)	2,100 ✓	2,000 ✓			
	14500 @ 1.75 = 25375		Opening inventory of finished goods	4,000	7,000
Purchases	15,500	27,125			
Sub-total	17,600	29,125			
Used	16,600	27.375	Cost of production	30,000	ADD TO
Closing inventory	1,000	1750	Materials		27.375

Closing inventory to be valued at budgeted purchase price

Labour — 26400

Overhead — 6225

Total — 60,000

Labour	Hours	£
Basic time @ £12 per hour	1600	19200
Overtime	400	7200
Total	2000	26400

$\frac{60,000}{30,000} = £2.00$ PER UNIT

Closing inventory of finished goods* — 5,000 — 10,000 DEDUCT

*Valued at budgeted production cost per unit

Cost of goods sold — OP. STOCK + COSTS − CL. STOCK — 57.000

It takes 4 minutes to make each item

8 staff work 200 basic hours each

Overtime is paid time and a half (50% above basic rate)

Gross profit — 18400

Workings schedules			Operating budget	Units	£
			Overheads		
			Administration		3,000
Overhead	**Hours**	**£**	Marketing		4,000
Variable @ £1.50 per hour	*2000*	*3000*	Total		7,000
Fixed		3,225			
Total		*6225*	Operating profit		*11400*

Variable overhead recovered on total labour hours

....

Task 1.4A

This year sales are £1,000,000.

Analysis of recent years shows a growth trend of 5% per annum.

The seasonal variation has been:

- Quarter 1   +£25,000
- Quarter 2   +£10,000
- Quarter 3   −£15,000
- Quarter 4   −£20,000

Forecast the income for each quarter of <u>next year</u>.

Quarter	£
1	*287.500*
2	*272 500*
3	*247 500*
4	*242.500*
Year	*1050 000*

....

Task 1.4B

Calculate these sales and cost budgets for April.

	Budget for the year	Budget for April
Units sold	24,000	2,000
Units produced	25,000	2,500
	£	£
Sales	480,000	40,000
Materials used	80,000	8000
Labour	64,800	6900
Variable production overhead	30,000	3000
Fixed overhead	1,800	150

Each unit is made from 2 kg of material costing £1.60 per kg. 2500 x 2 x 1.60

It takes 12 minutes to make each item.

350 hours of basic time is available in the month. Any extra hours must be worked in overtime.

The basic rate is £12 per hour. Overtime is paid at time and a half (50% more than basic rate). 350 x 12 = 4200 150 x 18 = 2700

Variable overhead relates to labour hours, including overtime. 30,000 ÷ 25,000 x 2500

Fixed overhead costs are incurred evenly through the year.

Task 1.4C

Prepare the cash forecast for May from the following budget data

Budget data	March £	April £	May £	June £	Cash forecast	May £
Invoiced sales	3,000	3,500	3,300	3,800	Opening cash balance	(480)
		1500 + 1750 = 3250				
Purchases	1,000	1,100	1,200	1,100	Customer receipts	*3250*
Wages	500	510	520	480		
Other overheads	600	660	620	630	**Payments**	
Capital expenditure	0	1,200	0	0	For purchases	*1000*
					For wages	*520*
Average terms					For overheads	*660*
Half of customers take 1 month to pay. Half take 2 months.					For capital exp.	*0*
Purchases paid for after two months					Total	*2180*
Wages paid in the current month						
Other overheads paid after one month					Closing cash balance	*590*
Capital expenditure paid in the current month					Show payments and receipts as plus figures.	
					Negative balance = overdrawn	

---

*RECOMMEND WEEKLY REVIEW OF PERFORMANCE BASED
ON: MINUTES PER UNIT
HOURS OF OVERTIME
PERCENTAGE OF GOOD OUTPUT
AVERAGE HOURLY RATE
SHOULD ALSO COMMISSION AN EMPLOYEE SATISFACTION
AND INVOLVEMENT QUESTIONNAIRE*

Task 1.5

You have prepared a draft budget for direct labour costs.

- It is based on this year's costs plus an expected pay rise and increased staffing.
- The manager of human resources has forecast the pay rise.
- You have calculated the required staffing from the agreed production budget.
- You have been asked to suggest appropriate performance measures that would assist managers to monitor direct labour performance against budget.

Direct labour budget

	This year	Next year budget
Production units	780,000	800,000
Minutes per unit	3.00	3.00
Labour hours	39,000	40,000
Annual hours per staff member	1,800	1,800
Number of staff	22	23
Average salary p.a.	£25,000	£26,500
Direct labour cost	£550,000	£609,500

Write an email to the Production Director:

(a) **Explaining the calculations and assumptions and requesting his approval.**

(b) **Suggesting appropriate direct labour performance indicators for this department.**

BUDGET SUBMISSION

I ATTACH PROPOSED DIRECT LABOUR BUDGET FOR NEXT YEAR FOR YOUR CONSIDERATION AND APPROVAL

THE AGREED PRODUCTION PLAN INDICATES AN INCREASE IN VOLUME TO 800,000 UNITS NEXT YR. NO CHANGE IN PRODUCTIVITY HAS BEEN ASSUMED, THEREFORE, STAFFING LEVELS NEED TO INCREASE BY 1 TO 23

THE HR MANAGER ESTIMATES AN. PAY INCREASE BY 6% TO £26,500

PLEASE LET ME KNOW IF YOU NEED FURTHER INFO

PERFORMANCE INDICATORS

THERE IS RANGE OF MEASURES TO MONITOR COST, EFFICIENCY, EFFECTIVENESS & EMPLOYEE SATISFACTION STAFF HOURS & OUTPUT DATA AVAILABLE DAILY. LABOUR RATES REVIEWED PERIODICALLY, HOWEVER, EMPLOYEE SATISFACTION BEST CANVASSED 1 OR 2 X P.A

To	Production Director	Date	(Today)
From	Budget Accountant	Subject	Review of Operation Statement

Budget submission

Performance indicators

Task 1.6A

The company has budgeted to make and sell 100,000 units in the coming year.

Each unit takes 0.5 labour hours to make and requires 2kg of raw material. The quality control department can test 8,000 units each month. A contract has been placed to purchase 150,000kg of raw material at an agreed price. Further supplies can be obtained on the open market but the price is likely to be much higher. The company employs 25 production workers. Each worker works 1,750 hours a year in normal time.

[handwritten: 25 × 1750 / 0.5 = 87500]

[handwritten: 50,000 − 43,750 =]

Complete the following analysis.

There is labour available to make *[handwritten: 87,500]* units in normal time. Therefore, *[handwritten: 6250]* hours of overtime will be needed.

[handwritten: 150000 / 2 =]

The raw material contract will provide enough material to make *[handwritten: 75000]* units. Therefore, *[handwritten: 50,000]* kg will have to be purchased on the open market.

Quality control can test *[handwritten: 96000]* units in the year. It will be necessary to make alternative arrangements for *[handwritten: 4000]* units.

....

Task 1.6B

From the following data, revise the income forecast.

Next year income is forecast at £7,350,000. This assumes a 5% increase in selling price.

In the light of increasing competition the marketing manager has decided not to make the increase.

The forecast should be revised to _____ *[handwritten: 7,000,000]* .

Select from:

- £6,982,500
- £7,000,000 *[circled]*
- £7,350,000
- £7,717,500

[handwritten: 7,350,000 / 105 × 100]

....

Task 1.6C

From the following data, revise the forecast for energy costs.

Next year, energy costs are forecast at £228,800. This assumes a 4% increase in energy consumption and a 5% increase in gas and electricity tariffs.

However, energy saving measures are being proposed. Instead of increasing, consumption should be reduced by 10%.

The energy budget should be £_____ .

Select from:

- £178,200
- £198,000 *[handwritten: — ?]*
- £217,800
- £220,000

....

[handwritten: 228,800 / (1.04 × 1.05) = 209,523.80]

Section 2

Task 2.1

A monthly operating statement is shown below with some explanatory notes. You are required to flex the budget, calculate variances and show whether each variance is favourable or adverse.

Monthly operating statement			Monthly operating statement			
	Budget	**Actual**	Volume	68,000		
Volume	63,000	68,000		**Flexed Budget**	**Actual**	**Varian Fav/(A**
	£	£		£	£	£
Revenue (turnover)	2,520,000	2,856,000	Revenue (turnover)	2,720,000	2,856,000	136,0
Costs			**Costs**			
Material	441,000	510,000	Material	476,000	510,000	(34,000
Labour	567,000	616,250	Labour	612000	616,250	(4250
Distribution	6,300	7,000	Distribution	6800	7,000	(200
Energy	151,000	164,000	Energy	161000	164,000	(3000
Equipment hire	32,000	35,000	Equipment hire	36,000	35,000	100
Depreciation	182,000	180,000	Depreciation	182000	180,000	2000
Marketing	231,000	235,000	Marketing	231,000	235,000	(4000
Administration	186,000	189,000	Administration	186,000	189,000	(3000
Total	1,796,300	1,936,250	Total	1,890,800	1,936,250	(45450
Operating profit	723,700	919,750	Operating profit	829,200	919,750	90350

Enter adverse variances as minus

Notes

Material, labour and distribution costs are variable.

The budget for energy is semi-variable. The variable element is £2.00 per unit.

The budget for equipment hire is stepped, increasing at every 8,000 units of monthly production.

Depreciation, marketing and administration costs are fixed.

∙∙∙

Task 2.2

You are asked to review the operating statement shown below, and the background information provided, and to make recommendations.

Operating statement for May			
Revenue (turnover) (units)	1,360,000		

	Budget	Actual	Variance
			Fav/(Adverse)
	£	£	£
Revenue (turnover)	2,720,000	2,992,000	272,000
Variable costs			
Material	816,000	884,000	(68,000)
Labour	612,000	571,200	40,800
Distribution	108,800	111,100	(2,300)
Power	136,000	138,000	(2,000)
Equipment hire	68,000	67,500	500
	1,740,800	1,771,800	(31,000)
Contribution	979,200	1,220,200	241,000
Fixed costs			
Power	14,000	15,000	(1,000)
Equipment hire	10,000	9,000	1,000
Depreciation	108,000	110,000	(2,000)

Operating statement for May			
Marketing	121,000	128,000	(7,000)
Administration	147,000	151,000	(4,000)
	400,000	413,000	(13,000)
Operating profit	579,200	807,200	228,000

The budget has been flexed to the actual number of units produced and sold. The original budget had been drawn up by the Chief Executive and communicated to senior managers by email.

Despite an unbudgeted price increase, the volume of units sold was higher than expected in the original budget. This seems to have been due to a very successful advertising campaign. Temporary staff had been recruited to avoid overtime costs.

One of the component parts of the product is made from brass which increased in price by 6% for part of the month.

Although pleased with the overall results, the Chief Executive is concerned that costs were above budget and has asked you to advise how control can be improved.

Write an email to the Chief Executive in which you:

(a) **Suggest possible reasons for the variances on materials, labour, marketing and administration**

(b) **Make recommendations on how cost accountability could be improved when setting budgets**

To	Chief Executive	Date	(Today)
From	Budget Accountant	Subject	Review of Operation Statement

Reasons for variances

Improving budget accountability

SAMPLE ASSESSMENT 1
BUDGETING

ANSWERS

Budgeting – answers to practice questions

Section 1

Task 1.1A

Data	Answer
Inflation trends in UK	Office for National Statistics
Value Added Tax (VAT) rates	HMRC publications
Demand for our products	Market Research

Task 1.1B

Situation	Answer
You want to identify the production capacity of the firm.	Production planning manager
You want to forecast the price of raw materials.	Buyer
The draft budget is ready for review.	Budget committee

Task 1.1C

Personnel
Printing recruitment application forms

Cost of production
Production wages
Raw material usage

Maintenance
Spare parts for production machines

> **Capital expenditure**
>
> Warehouse extension

> **Marketing**
>
> Advertising
>
> Customer demand survey
>
> Commission paid to sales staff

Task 1.1D

Situation	Answer
Holiday pay for production workers	Charge to production in a labour hour overhead rate
Material wastage in the production process	Direct cost
Cost of the purchasing department	Activity based charge to production cost centres
Administrative wages	Allocate to administrative overheads
Computing services	Allocate to administrative overheads
Production equipment maintenance	Charge to production in a machine hour overhead rate
Depreciation of production equipment	Charge to production in a machine hour overhead rate
Redecoration of the sales showroom	Allocate to marketing overheads

---

Task 1.1E

Overhead recovery should be based on **Labour hours**. The recovery rate will be £2 per **hour**.

Task 1.2A

Units of product P

	Week 1	Week 2	Week 3	Week 4	Week 5
Opening inventory (stock)	1,200	1,500	1,350	1,650	
Production	6,300	4,850	4,800	5,950	
Sub-total	7,500	6,350	6,150	7,600	
Sales	6,000	5,000	4,500	5,500	7,000
Closing inventory (stock)	1,500	1,350	1,650	2,100	

....

Task 1.2B

	Month 1	Month 2	Month 3
Required units	72,000	90,000	81,000
Manufactured units (required x 100/90)	80,000	100,000	90,000

....

Task 1.2C

23,000m

Working

15,000 items @ 1,5 metres   =   22,500m

22,500m x 100 / 90 (wastage) =   25,000

Less 2,000m inventory (stock) reduction = 23,000m

....

Task 1.2D

300

Working

36,000 x 5/60   =   3,000 hrs basic time

3,000 – (15 x 180)   =   300 hrs overtime

....

Task 1.2E

Product	Units	Hours per Unit	Hours required
A	140	1.5	210
B	210	2.0	420
C	170	3.0	510
Total hours for department X			1,140

How many additional machines should be hired?

((1,140 – (3 x 250))/250 = 1.56, round up to 2

2

Task 1.2F

Workings schedules			Operating budget	Units	£
Materials	**Kg**	**£**	Sales revenue @ £2.60 each	29,000	75,400
Opening inventory (stock)	2,100	2,000			
Purchases	15,500	27,125	Opening inventory of finished goods	4,000	7,000
Sub-total	17,600	29,125			
Used	16,600	27,375	Cost of production	30,000	
Closing inventory	1,000	1,750	Materials		27,375
Closing inventory to be valued at budgeted purchase price			Labour		26,400
			Overhead		6,225
			Total		60,000

148

Workings schedules			Operating budget	Units	£

Labour

	Hours	£
Basic time @ £12 per hour	1,600	19,200
Overtime	400	7,200
Total	2,000	26,400

It takes 4 minutes to make each item

8 staff work 200 basic hours each

Overtime is paid time and a half (50% above basic rate)

Overhead

	Hours	£
Variable @ £1.50 per hour	2,000	3,000
Fixed		3,225
Total		6,225

Variable overhead recovered on total labour hours

Operating budget	Units	£
Closing inventory of finished goods*	5,000	10,000
*Valued at budgeted production cost per unit		
Cost of goods sold		57,000
Gross profit		18,400
Overheads		
Administration		3,000
Marketing		4,000
Total		7,000
Operating profit		11,400

Task 1.4A

Quarter	£
1	287,500
2	272,500
3	247,500
4	242,500
Year	1,050,000

Task 1.4B

	Budget for April
Units sold	2,000
Units produced	2,500
	£
Sales	40,000
Materials used	8,000
Labour	6,900
Variable production overhead	3,000
Fixed overhead	150

Task 1.4C

Cash forecast	May
	£
Opening cash balance	(480)

Customer receipts	3,250

Payments

For purchases	1,000
For wages	520
For overheads	660
For capital exp.	0
Total	2,180

Closing cash balance	590

Task 1.5

To: Production Director

From: Accounting Assistant

Date: xx/xx/xxxx

Subject: Direct Labour Budget

Budget submission

I attach the proposed direct labour budget for next year for your consideration and approval.

The agreed production plan indicates an increase in volume to 800,000 units next year. No change in productivity has been assumed. Therefore, the staffing level needs to increase by one to 23.

The manager of human resources estimates that average pay will increase by 6% next year to £26,500.

Please let me know if you need any further information.

Performance indicators

There is a range of useful measures to monitor cost, efficiency, effectiveness, and employee satisfaction. Staff hours and output data should be available on a daily basis. Labour rates are reviewed periodically. However, employee satisfaction is probably best canvassed once or twice a year. I recommend that we conduct a weekly review of performance based on:

- Minutes per unit
- Hours of overtime
- Percentage of good output (or similar quality measure)
- Average hourly rate

We should also commission a confidential employee satisfaction and involvement questionnaire.

A Technician

Task 1.6A

There is labour available to make **87,500** units in normal time. Therefore, **6,250** hours of overtime will be needed.

The raw material contract will provide enough material to make **75,000** units. Therefore, **50,000** kg will have to be purchased on the open market.

Quality control can test **96,000** units in the year. It will be necessary to make alternative arrangements for **4,000** units.

Task 1.6B

The forecast should be revised to **£7,000,000**.

Task 1.6C

The energy budget should be **£198,000**.

Section 2

Task 2.1

Monthly operating statement

Volume   68,000

	Flexed Budget	Actual	Variance Fav/(Adv)
	£	£	£
Revenue (turnover)	2,720,000	2,856,000	136,000
Costs			
Material	476,000	510,000	(34,000)
Labour	612,000	616,250	(4,250)
Distribution	6,800	7,000	(200)
Energy	161,000	164,000	(3,000)
Equipment hire	36,000	35,000	1,000
Depreciation	182,000	180,000	2,000
Marketing	231,000	235,000	(4,000)
Administration	186,000	189,000	(3,000)
Total	1,890,800	1,936,250	(45,450)
Operating profit	829,200	919,750	90,550

Task 2.2

To	Chief Executive	Date	(Today)
From	Budget Accountant	Subject	Review of Operating Statement

Reasons for variances

I have reviewed the results for May. Profit in the month was £807,200 driven by a 10% price improvement over budget and increased volume. After flexing the original budget to allow for the increased volume, we are reporting adverse expense variances of £44,000.

The only significant favourable expense variance is labour. This is one cost which you might expect to be adverse because increased workloads tend to create high overtime costs. This was avoided by using temporary workers and cost savings were made.

Material costs were 8% over budget. The increase in brass costs does not adequately explain this variance. We need to investigate whether the use of temporary workers, and the demotivating impact of this on the permanent staff, may have led to higher levels of material wastage. It may be preferable to use our own staff at overtime rates.

Marketing costs were £7,000 over budget, no doubt due to the costs of the advertising campaign, and this seems to be money well spent.

The administration overspend is worrying and needs to be investigated. It could have been a one-off. Alternatively, perhaps there are variable costs such as overtime or bonus that should not have been budgeted as fixed costs.

Improving budget accountability

Budgets are useful for planning, coordination, authorisation and control. However, this requires the full and enthusiastic involvement of the management team. I suggest that you need to:

- Involve the whole team in the planning process.
- Insist that all known factors and plans (such as the advertising campaign) are built into the budget.
- Assign responsibilities to individuals for all aspect of the budget.
- Allow managers freedom to manage their budgets.

SAMPLE ASSESSMENT 2
BUDGETING

Time allowed: 2 hours 30 minutes

Section 1

Task 1.1A

Match the data in the first column with the appropriate source in the second column.

Data   **Source**

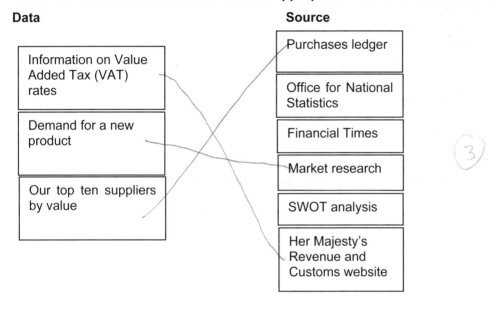

Data	Source
Information on Value Added Tax (VAT) rates	Purchases ledger
Demand for a new product	Office for National Statistics
Our top ten suppliers by value	Financial Times
	Market research
	SWOT analysis
	Her Majesty's Revenue and Customs website

③

Task 1.1B

Whom would you contact in each of the following situations?

You want to explain a labour rate variance ....HR. MANAGER........

You want to explain a labour efficiency variance ....PRODUCTION MANAGER

You want to forecast next year's sales revenue ..MARKETING DIRECTOR..

Choose from:

③

Advertising department

Human resources manager

Marketing director

Budget committee

Production manager

Task 1.1C

Take each item of cost in the list below and place it into its appropriate budget

Item of cost

Maintenance cost of delivery vehicles
Factory extension
Factory rent and heating costs
Order for production materials
Servicing of computers
Salaries of sales personnel
Advertising costs
Printing of application forms

Appropriate budget

Capital expenditure
FACTORY EXTENSION

Sales and marketing
SALARIES OF SALES
ADVERTISING

Distribution
MAINTENANCE OF
DELIVERY VEHICLES

Cost of production
FACTORY RENT
PRODUCTION MATS

Finance and administration
SERVICE OF COMPUTERS
PRINTING

Task 1.1D

Select an appropriate accounting treatment for each of the following costs.

Cost	Accounting treatment
Administration wages	ADMIN O/H ✓
Depreciation of delivery vehicles	DISTRIB O/H ✓
Overtime pay for production workers	LABOUR HOUR O/H. ✓
Repair of office computers	ADMIN O/H. ✓
Printing of leaflets for new product	MARKET O/H ✓
Maintenance of production equipment	M/C HOUR O/H ✓
Hiring of specialised machine for production	DIRECT ✓
Mobile phones for sales staff	MARKET ✓

Options available are:

Allocate to distribution overheads

Charge to production in a machine hour overhead rate

Charge to production in a labour hour overhead rate

Allocate to administrative overheads

Allocate to marketing overheads

Direct cost

....

Task 1.1E

Calculate the appropriate budgeted overhead recovery rate for the following production department.

The department's annual budget for indirect costs is:

Cost	£
Indirect labour	16,000
Supervisor wages	58,000
Depreciation of equipment	10,000
Machine maintenance	5,000
Pension contributions	11,000
Total	100,000

Notes

The department makes two different products and the labour and machine time required per unit of each product differs. The budgeted production of 40,000 units will require 2,000 machine hours and 25,000 direct labour hours.

Overhead recovery should be based on **Labour hours / Machine hours / Units produced**.

The recovery will be £ 4 per **Labour hour / Machine hour / Unit produced**

Task 1.2A

Complete the following production forecast for product P.

Closing inventory (stock) should be 25% of forecast sales for the following week.

	Week 1	Week 2	Week 3	Week 4	Week 5
Opening inventory (stock)	3,400	3000	2400	2800	3000
Production	13600	11400	10000	11400	
Sub-total	17000	14400	12400	14200	
Sales	14,000	12,000	9,600	11,200	12,000
Closing inventory (stock)	3000	2400	2800	3000	

Task 1.2B

The quarterly production requirements for product L are shown below.

15% of production fails the quality checks and must be scrapped.

How many items of product L must be manufactured each month to allow for waste?

	Month 1	Month 2	Month 3
Required units	170,000	187,000	153,000
Manufactured units	200,000	220,000	180,000

Task 1.2C

50,000 items of product M are to be manufactured in April.

Each requires 10 metres of raw material.

20% of raw material is wasted during manufacture.

The opening inventory (stock) will be 4,000 metres.

The closing inventory (stock) will be 6,000 metres.

How much material must be purchased in April?

627,000 metres ☑

627,500 metres ☐

628,750 metres ☐

630,000 metres ☐

632,500 metres ☐

Task 1.2D

10,000 items of product N are to be manufactured in May.

Each one takes 15 minutes to produce. 2500 HRS

12 staff will each work 200 basic hours. 2400 HRS

How many overtime hours must be worked to complete the production?

2,500 hours ☐

100 hours ☑

300 hours ☐

2,400 hours ☐

200 hours ☐

Task 1.2E

Department X manufactures three products: A, B and C.

Calculate the machine hours needed to manufacture these products in November.

Product	Units	Hours per unit	Hours required
A	600	1.5	900
B	500	3.0	1500
C	700	2.0	1400
Total			3800

✓

There are 8 machines in the department.

Additional machines can be hired if required.

Each machine can be used for 325 hours in December.

How many additional machines should be hired?

4   ✓

....

Task 1.3

You are required to complete the operating budget below.

This is the production budget.

Production budget	Units
Opening inventory (stock) of finished goods	3,000
Production	39,000
Sub-total	42,000
Sales	38,000
Closing inventory (stock) of finished goods	4,000

....

Complete these three working schedules.

Enter the missing figures in the working schedules.

Materials
Each unit produce requires 0.8kg of material.

Closing inventory (stock) will be valued at the budgeted purchase price.

Materials	Kg	£
Opening inventory (stock)	1,400	3,300
Purchases	31,000	77,500
Sub-total	32,400	80,800
Used in production	31,200 ✓	77800 ✓
Closing inventory (stock)	1200 ✓	3000 ✓

Labour

It takes 5 minutes to make each item. 3250 HRS

14 staff work 200 basic hours each. 2800 HRS

Overtime is paid at 35% above the basic hourly rate.

Labour	Hours	£
Basic time @ £10 per hour	2800 ✓	28000 ✓
Overtime	450	6075
Total	3250	34075 ✓

Overhead

Variable overhead is recovered on total labour hours.

Overhead	Hours	£
Variable @ £0.9 per hour	3250 ✓	2925 ✓
Fixed		4,150
Total		7075 ✓

Now complete the operating budget.

Closing inventory (stock) will be valued at the budgeted total cost of production per unit.

Enter the missing figures in the operating budget.

Operating budget	Units	£ per unit	£
Sales	38,000	5.10	193 800
Cost of goods sold:			
Opening inventory (stock) of finished goods			7,000
Cost of production		£	
Materials		77 800	
Labour		34 075	
Overhead		70 75	
Total cost of production			118 950
Closing inventory (stock) of finished goods 4000 x		$\frac{118.950}{39,000}$	12 200
Cost of goods sold			113 750
Gross profit			80,050
Overheads:			
Administration		2,800	
Marketing		3,800	
Total overheads			6600
Net profit			73450

Task 1.4A

This year sales are £700,000. Analysis of recent years shows a growth trend of 4% per year.

The seasonal variation has been:

quarter 1	−£6,000
quarter 2	−£2,000
quarter 3	+£9,000
quarter 4	−£1,000

722,006

182,000

Forecast the income for each quarter of next year.

Quarter	£
1	176,000 ✓
2	180,000
3	191,000
4	181,000 ✓
Year	728,000

....

Task 1.4B

Calculate sales and cost budgets for May from the following data.

Budgeted units	Year	May
Units sold	55,000	4,500
Units produced	58,000	4,800

Each unit is made from 2 kg of material costing £3 per kg. *£ 348,000*

58,000 × 2kg × 3

It takes 12 minutes to make each item.

700 hours of basic labour time is available in the month. Any extra hours must be worked in overtime.

The basic rate is £12 per hour. Overtime is paid at 25% above basic rate.

Variable overhead relates to labour hours, including overtime.

Fixed overhead costs are incurred evenly through the year.

11600 hrs   *960 Hrs*

700 @ 12   *700 @ 12   8600*
46   *260 @ 15   3900*
              12300

Sample assessment 2: questions

Budget in £	Year	May		
Sales	605,000	49500 ✓		
Material used	348,000	28 800		
Direct labour	148,800	12.300 ✓		
Variable production overhead	9,280	768	767 ?	
Fixed overhead	4,800	400 ✓		

$$\frac{12300}{148800} \times 9280 = 767$$

Task 1.4C

Prepare a cash forecast for May from the following data.

Budget data	March £	April £	May £	June £
Invoiced sales	9,000	9,250	9,100	9,400
urchases	4,100	3,800	3,100	3,650
Wages	1,050	1,250	1,100	1,250
Other overheads	2,200	2,300	2,400	2,040
Capital expenditure	4,000	0	0	4,000

Average terms

Customers take 1 month to pay.

Purchases are paid for after 2 months.
Wages are paid in the current month.
Other overheads are paid for after 1 month.
Capital expenditure is paid for after 1 month.

Cash forecast	£
Opening cash balance	1,255
Customer receipts	9250 ✓
Payments	✓
Purchases	4100
Wages	1100
Overheads	2300
Capital expenditure	0
Total	7500
Closing cash balance	3005

Notes

A negative figure = an overdraft

Enter payments as positive figures.

••

Task 1.5

You have prepared a draft budget for direct material costs.

– The material used is cotton which is imported from a regular source in India.

– It is based on this year's costs plus an expected increase in material prices.

– The manager of the purchasing department has forecast the price rise.

– You have calculated the required material from the agreed forecast production budget. An allowance has been made for wastage.

– You have been asked to describe how the impact of factors in the external environment and any specific external costs on budgets could affect the budget forecast.

Direct material budget	This year actual	Next year budget
Production units	700,000	750,000
Required material per unit	1 kg	1 kg
Material purchased	736,842 kg	789,474 kg
Price per kg	£3.00	£3.30
Total cost of material	£2,210,526	£2,605,264

Write an email to the Production Director:

(a) **Explaining the calculations and assumptions and requesting his approval.**

(b) **Describing how the impact of external factors in the environment and any specific external costs could affect the budget forecast.**

Answer

To	Production Director	From	Budget Accountant
Subject	Direct material budget	Date	XX XX XX

(a) **Explanation on budget submission**

(b) **Impact of external environment and other specific external costs**

Budget Accountant

Task 1.6

A company makes and sells a single product. A first draft operating budget has been prepared for next year. The Marketing Director has suggested that profit might be improved by increasing the selling price, even though volume would fall.

(a) **You are asked to prepare a revised operating budget in the Revision column below and calculate the increase or decrease in profit that would result.**

You should assume that the selling price will be increased by 5% and sales volume will fall by 10%.

Draft operating budget	First draft	Revision
Sales units	140,000	126,000
	£	£
Sales price	14.00	14.70
Sales value	1,960,000	1852,200
Variable production costs	1,120,000	1008000
Fixed production costs	420,000	420,000
Gross profit	420,000	424,200
Gross profit will increase/decrease by		4200

(b) The draft administration salary budget is £195,700. This assumes a 3% pay rise from the first day of the year. The administration manager has decided to increase this to 5%.

Calculate the revised salary budget £ | 199500 |

(c) This year's budget for raw materials was set at £216,300. This assumed a 3% increase in production volume and a 5% increase in raw material prices compared with the previous year.

However production volume is 10% higher than the previous year and there has been no price increase.

Calculate the material cost forecast £ | 220,000 |

....

$$\frac{216,300}{1.03 \times 1.05} = 200,000 \times 1.1 = 220,000$$

Section 2

Task 2.1

You are required to complete a monthly operating report for June from the data provided.

The budget for the month is provided with some notes.

Operating budget for June	£
Sales (65,000 units)	2,600,000
Costs	
Material	455,000
Labour	585,000
Distribution	6,500
Energy	150,000
Equipment hire	33,000
Depreciation	182,000
Marketing	225,000
Administration	186,000
Total	1,822,500
Operating profit	777,500

Notes

Material, labour and distribution costs are variable.

Energy cost is semi-variable. The variable element is budgeted at £2.00 per unit of sales.

Equipment hire is a stepped cost, budgeted to increase at every 6,000 units of monthly production.

Depreciation, marketing and administration costs are fixed.

You are required to flex the budget, calculate variances and show whether each variance is favourable or adverse. The actual results have been entered for you.

Operating report for June	Flexed budget £	Actual £	Variance + or –£
Sales (70,000 units)	2,800,000	2,940,000	-140.000
Costs			
Material	490.000	525,000	-35.000
Labour	630,000	634,375	- 4.375
Distribution	7000	7,206	- 206
Energy	160000	160,000	0
Equipment hire	36.000	36,000	0
Depreciation	182.000	180,000	2000
Marketing	225.000	230,000	-5000
Administration	186,000	189,000	-3000
Total costs	1,916,000	1,961,581	-45581
Operating profit	884000	978,419	94419

Enter zeroes where appropriate and enter adverse variances as negative. For example: −500.

Enter a loss as negative. For example: −500.

Task 2.2

You are asked to review the operating statement for May and the background information provided below, and to make recommendations.

Operating statement	Flexed budget £ '000s	Actual £ '000s	Variance £ '000s Fav/(Adv)
Sales (1,300,000 units)	2,600	2,860	260
Variable costs			
Material	780	845	(65)
Labour	585	546	39
Distribution	104	106	(2)
Power	130	132	(2)
Equipment hire	68	67	1
Total	1,667	1,696	(29)
Contribution	933	1,164	231
Fixed costs			
Power	13	14	(1)
Depreciation	100	102	(2)
Marketing	116	123	(7)
Administration	140	144	(4)
Total	369	383	(14)
Operating profit	564	781	217

Background information

The budget has been flexed to the actual number of units produced and sold. Despite an unbudgeted price increase, the volume of units sold was higher than expected in the original budget. This seems to have been due to a very successful advertising campaign. Temporary staff had been recruited to avoid overtime costs. One of the component parts of the product is made from brass which increased in price by 5%.

Although pleased with the overall results, the chief executive is concerned that costs were above budget and feels that the results could have been improved by better budgetary control.

Write an email to the chief executive in which you:

(a) **Suggest possible reasons for the variances on materials, labour, marketing and administration.**

(b) **Justify the uses of budgetary control for planning, co-ordination, authorisation and cost control.**

To	The Chief Executive	From	Budget Accountant	
Subject	Review of Operating Statement	Date	XX XX XX	

(a) **Reason for variances**

(b) **Justification for the uses of budgetary control**

Budget Accountant

SAMPLE ASSESSMENT 2
BUDGETING

ANSWERS

Section 1

Task 1.1A

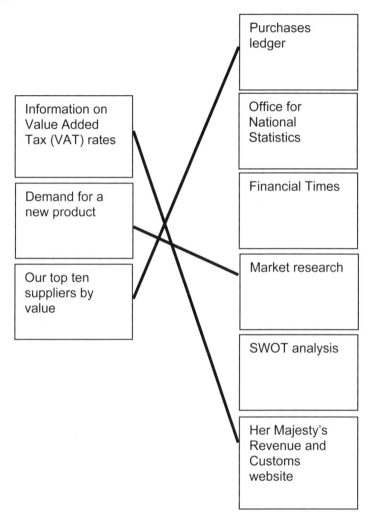

Task 1.1B

You want to explain a labour rate variance   **Human resources manager**

You want to explain a labour efficiency variance   **Production manager**

You want to forecast next year's sales revenue   **Marketing director**

Task 1.1C

Capital expenditure
Factory extension

Sales and marketing
Salaries of sales personnel
Advertising costs

Distribution
Maintenance cost of delivery vehicles

Cost of production
Factory rent and heating costs
Order for production materials

Finance and administration
Servicing of computers
Printing of application forms

Task 1.1D

Cost	Accounting treatment
Administration wages	Allocate to administrative overheads
Depreciation of delivery vehicles	Allocate to distribution overheads
Overtime pay for production workers	Charge to production in a labour hour overhead
Repair of office computers	Allocate to administrative overheads
Printing of leaflets for new product	Allocate to marketing overheads
Maintenance of production equipment	Charge to production in a machine hour overhead
Hiring of specialised machine for production	Direct cost
Mobile phones for sales staff	Allocate to marketing overheads

Task 1.1E

Overhead recovery should be based on **labour hours**.

The recovery rate will be (£100,000/25,000) = **£4** per **labour hour**.

Task 1.2A

	Week 1	Week 2	Week 3	Week 4	Week 5
Opening inventory (stock)	3,400	3,000	2,400	2,800	
Production (bal fig)	13,600	11,400	10,000	11,400	
Sub-total	17,000	14,400	12,400	14,200	
Sales	14,000	12,000	9,600	11,200	12,000
Closing inventory (stock)	3,000	2,400	2,800	3,000	

Task 1.2B

	Month 1	Month 2	Month 3
Required units	170,000	187,000	153,000
Manufactured units (required x 100/85)	200,000	220,000	180,000

Task 1.2C

Answer: **627,000 metres**

Working

		Metres
Required for good production	50,000 x 10	500,000
Wastage	500,000 x 20/80	125,000
Total required		625,000
Add: closing inventory		6,000
Less: opening inventory		(4,000)
Total materials		627,000

Task 1.2D

Answer: **100 hours** ((10,000 x 15/60) – (12 x 200) = 100)

Task 1.2E

Calculate the machine hours needed to manufacture these in November.

Product	Units	Hours per unit	Hours required
A	600	1.5	900
B	500	3.0	1,500
C	700	2.0	1,400
Total			3,800

Eight machines operating for 325 hours means that 2,600 machine hours can be supplied in-house, so (3,800 – 2,600)/325 = 3.69 machines should be hired, rounded up to **4** additional machines.

Task 1.3

Materials	kg	£
Opening inventory (stock)	1,400	3,300
Purchases	31,000	77,500
Sub-total	32,400	80,800
Used in production	31,200	77,800
Closing inventory (stock)	1,200	3,000

Working

39,000 x 0.8kg = 31,200 kg will be used in production, leaving 32,400 – 31,200 = 1,200 kgs in inventory. These are valued at £77,500/31,000 = £2.50 each, that is at £3,000.

Labour	Hours	£
Basic time @ £10 per hour	2,800	28,000
Overtime	450	6,075
Total	3,250	34,075

Working

39,000 x 5/60 = 3,250 labour hours are required in total but only 14 x 200 = 2,800 basic hours are available, so 3,250 – 2,800 = 450 hours must be paid at overtime rates: 450 x £10 x 1.35 = £6,075.

Overhead	Hours	£
Variable @ £0.9 per hour	3,250	2,925
Fixed		4,150
Total		7,075

Operating budget	Units	£ per unit	£
Sales	38,000	5.10	193,800
Cost of goods sold:			
Opening inventory (stock) of finished goods			7,000
Cost of production		£	
Materials		77,800	
Labour		34,075	
Overhead		7,075	
Total cost of production			118,950
Closing inventory (stock) of finished goods (118,950/39,000 x 4,000)			12,200
Cost of goods sold			113,750
Gross profit			80,050
Overheads			
Administration		2,800	
Marketing		3,800	
Total overheads			6,600
Net profit			73,450

Task 1.4A

Quarter	£
1 ((700,000 x 1.04)/4) – 6,000	176,000
2 ((700,000 x 1.04)/4) – 2,000	180,000
3 ((700,000 x 1.04)/4) + 9,000	191,000
4 ((700,000 x 1.04)/4) – 1,000	181,000
Year (700,000 x 1.04)	728,000

Task 1.4B

Budget	Year £	May £
Sales 605,000/55,000 x 4,500	605,000	49,500
Material used 4,800 x 2 x £3	348,000	28,800
Direct labour (W)	148,800	12,300
Variable production overhead	9,280	767
Fixed overhead (4,800/12)	4,800	400

Workings

Labour: 4,800 x 12/60 = 960 hours needed for production, so 960 – 700 = 260 hours are at overtime rates.

Variable overhead: 12,300/148,800 x £9,280 = £767

		£
Basic hours	700 x £12	8,400
Overtime hours	260 x £12 x 1.25	3,900
Total cost		12,300

Task 1.4C

Cash forecast	£
Opening cash balance	1,255
Customer receipts (April sales)	9,250
Payments	
Purchases (March purchases)	4,100
Wages (May wages)	1,100
Overheads (April overheads)	2,300
Capital expenditure	0
Total	7,500
Closing cash balance	3,005

Task 1.5

To	Production Director	From	Budget Accountant
Subject	Direct material budget	Date	XX XX XX

Answer

(a) Explanation on budget submission

I attach the proposed direct material budget for next year for your consideration and approval.

The agreed production plan indicates an increase in volume to 750,000 units next year. It is assumed that this forecast is correct. It is also assumed that there will be no change to the material used per unit which represents an 36,842/700,000 x 100% = 5.3% wastage rate.

The purchasing manager estimates that the price of material will increase by 10% to £3.30 per kg.

Please let me know if you need any further information.

(b) Impact of external environment and other specific external costs

There are several factors in the external environment and other specific external costs which could affect the budget forecast.

Possibility of material price increases if there is a world shortage of cotton.

Impact of changes in the world economy, eg banking crisis, threat of bankruptcy in EU countries.

Rise in the price of oil affecting transport costs.

Can we guarantee that the quality will remain the same? If the quality of the material is poor, then more wastage will be incurred.

Can we rely on our source of supply?

Plus any other valid suggestions.

Budget Accountant

Task 1.6

(a)

Draft operating budget	First draft	Revision
Sales units (140,000 x 0.9)	140,000	126,000
	£	£
Sales price (14 x 1.05)	14.00	14.70
Sales value	1,960,000	1,852,200
Variable production costs (1,120,000 x 0.9)	1,120,000	1,008,000
Fixed production costs	420,000	420,000
Gross profit	420,000	424,200
Gross profit will **increase** by		4,200

(b) **Revised salary budget** £195,700 x 105/103 £199,500

(c) **Material cost forecast**   £ 220,000

Working

Let X be last year's amount. £216,300 = X x 1.03 x 1.05, so X = £216,300/(1.03 x 1.05) = £200,000. Therefore this year is £200,000 x 1.1 = £220,000

Section 2

Task 2.1

Operating report for June	Flexed budget £	Actual £	Variance + or −£
Sales (70,000 units)	2,800,000	2,940,000	140,000
Costs			
Material	490,000	525,000	−35,000
Labour	630,000	634,375	−4,375
Distribution	7,000	7,206	−206
Energy	160,000	160,000	0
Equipment hire	36,000	36,000	0
Depreciation	182,000	180,000	2,000
Marketing	225,000	230,000	−5,000
Administration	186,000	189,000	−3,000
Total costs	1,916,000	1,961,581	−45,581
Operating profit	884,000	978,419	94,419

Working

1   Sales £2,600,000/65,000 = £40 per unit, so flexed budget is 70,000 x £40 = 2,800,000

2   Materials £455,000/65,000 = £7 per unit, so flexed budget is 70,000 x £7 = 490,000

3   Labour £585,000/65,000 = £9 per unit, so flexed budget is 70,000 x £9 = 630,000

4   Distribution £6,500/65,000 = £0.10 per unit, so flexed budget is 70,000 x £0.10 = £7,000

5   Energy variable: 65,000 x £2 = £130,000, so fixed element is £150,000 - £130,000 = £20,000. Therefore flexed budget this year is (70,000 x £2) + £20,000 = £160,000

6   Equipment hire: 65,000/6,000 = 10.83, so 11 items were budgeted to be hired at £33,000/11 = £3,000 each. When production 70,000 units, 70,000/6,000 = 11.67 ie 12 items must be hired, at a cost of 12 x £3,000 = £36,000

Task 2.2

To	The Chief Executive	From	Budget Accountant
Subject	Review of operating statement	Date	XX XX XX

(a) Reasons for variances on materials, labour, marketing and administration

I have reviewed the results for May. Operating profit in the month was £781,000 driven by a 10% price improvement over budget (£2.20 versus £2) and increased volume. After flexing the original budget to allow for the increased volume we are reporting adverse expense variances of £43,000.

The only significant favourable expense variance is labour. This is one cost which you might expect to be adverse because increased workloads tend to create high overtime costs. This was avoided by using temporary workers and cost savings were made.

Material costs were 8.3% over budget. The increase in one of the component parts by 5% does not adequately explain this variance. We need to investigate whether the use of temporary workers, and the demotivating impact of this on the permanent staff, may have led to higher levels of material wastage. It may be preferable to use our own staff at overtime rates.

Marketing costs were £7,000 over budget, no doubt due to the costs of the advertising campaign, and this seems to be money well spent.

The administration overspend of £4,000 is worrying and needs to be investigated. It could have been a one-off. Alternatively, perhaps there are variable costs such as overtime or bonus that should not have been budgeted as fixed costs.

(b) Justification for the uses of budgetary control

Budgets are useful for planning, coordination, authorisation and cost control as outlined below.

Planning	The preparation of a budget enables management to look ahead, to plan how it will achieve its targets and the resources it needs to enable it to do so, thus having more control over its future.
Co-ordination	By involving and communicating to each person affected by the budget plans, this helps to maintain better overall control and also helps ensure that all departments are working towards the same goal.
Authorisation	Better budgetary control is achieved when responsibilities are assigned to individuals for all aspects of the budget as well as clear lines of authority for decision making.
Cost control	Producing budget forecasts enables the continuous process of comparing the actual results against the budget. This allows any departures from budget to be investigated and action taken where necessary.

Budget Accountant

PRACTICE ASSESSMENT 1
BUDGETING

Time allowed: 2 hours 30 minutes

Section 1

Task 1.1A

For each of the following tasks or activities, choose the appropriate department or function with responsibility for the task:

- Installation of anti-virus software on the computer system *IT* ✓
- Cash collection from customers and clients *FINANCE* ✓
- Preparing for the organisation's annual audit *FINANCE* ✓
- Advising employees on anti-discrimination laws *HR* ✓
- Setting up the organisation's private health insurance scheme *HR* ✓
- Collecting a petty cash float from the bank *FINANCE* ✓
- Repairing broken machinery *MAINTENANCE* ✓

Select from:

- HR (Human Resources)
- Finance
- IT
- Maintenance department

Task 1.1B

A school plans a trip to a local theatre for 30 pupils and teachers.

Classify each of the following costs in terms of its behaviour i.e. as variable, semi-variable or stepped.

- Hire of mini-buses which seat 12 people each *STEPPED* ✓
- Theatre tickets *VARIABLE* ✓
- Photocopying of permission letters to parents on the school photocopier which is rented. *SEMI-VARIABLE* ✓

Task 1.1C

Allocate the following costs and revenues to the responsibility centres in this business (as listed below)

- Client entertaining at horse racing MARKETING
- Repair of security alarm system in offices ADMIN
- Sick pay for production manager PRODUCTION
- Bonuses for sales managers SALES
- Depreciation of production equipment PRODUCTION
- Cost of recruiting new sales manager SALES

Select from:

- Production department
- Marketing department
- Administration department
- Sales team

....

Task 1.1D

- Classify the following items of expenditure as capital or revenue for budgeting purposes:
- Redecorating outside of head office building REVENUE
- Purchase of new machine CAPITAL
- Replacement of blades on cutting machine REVENUE
- Cost of hire-car for managing director to attend meeting in London REVENUE

....

Task 1.1E

Suggest, from the sources below, where a manager setting a budget would find the following information

- The cost of advertising in a local newspaper RATE CARD
- National insurance rates for the coming year HMREV
- Raw material costs INVOICES
- Costs of new equipment/machinery BROCHURES

Select from:

- HM Revenue & Customs
- Financial press
- Trade Association
- Prior period invoices
- Sales brochures
- Newspaper's rate card

....

Task 1.2A

Each unit takes 1.25 hours to produce. There are 20 workers, half of whom work 30 hours basic time a week and the other half work 40 hours basic time a week.

How many units can be produced during basic time in one week?

Select from:

- 1,400
- 1,120
- 700
- (560) ✓
- 875

Handwritten working:
$10 \times 30 = 300$
$10 \times 40 = 400$
700 HRS
$\frac{700}{1.25} = 560$

....

Task 1.2B

Materials cost is £1.20 per kg. The opening inventory (stock) of material is 34,500kg and this is required to fall by 20% by the end of the period. The materials usage budget is 168,000 kg. The budget for materials purchases is £...193,320...

Select from:

- £161,100
- £209,880
- £194,700
- (£193,320)
- £201,600

Handwritten working:
USE 168,000
+ 27,600
195,600
− 34,500
161,100 × 1.20 =

CLOSING
34,500
− 20%
27,600

Handwritten note:
↓ LEARN METHOD

Task 1.2C

Sales are forecast for the next three months as follows, for product A. The closing inventory (stock) figure should be 500 units more than the opening inventory (stock) figure per month.

Complete the table, assuming that each unit requires 15 minutes labour, and the labour cost is £10 per hour   SALES + CLOSING - OPENING = PROD.

	Month 1	Month 2	Month 3
Sales (units)	12,000	15,000	10,000
Opening inventory (stock) (units)	800	1300	1800
Production (balancing figure) (units)	12,500	15,500	10,500
Closing inventory (stock) (units)	1300	1800	2300
Labour cost (£)	31,250	38,750	26,250

Task 1.2D

One supervisor is required for every 200 labour hours worked in a week. A supervisor has a weekly wage of £500. The production budget shows production of 1,360 units in the forthcoming week. Each unit requires 30 minutes of labour time.

What is the budgeted supervisor cost for the forthcoming week?

$$\frac{1360}{2} = 680 \text{ HRS}$$

$$\frac{680}{200} = 4 \text{ SUPERS}$$

Select from:

- £500
- £1,500
- (£2,000) ✓
- £2,500
- £3,500

Task 1.2E

The following budget for a four week period is shown in total. Complete the budget for the individual weeks.

The total available basic labour time per week is 1,000 hours. Each unit requires 0.5 labour hours. The cost of labour is £8 per hour, or £10 per hour overtime.

Material costs are variable. Overheads are stepped, costing £500 in a week with a production up to 2,750 units and £1,000 per week above this.

	Total four weeks	Week 1	Week 2	Week 3	Week 4
Production and sales (units)	10,000	2,000	3,000	2,500	2,500
Material usage (£)	5,000	1000	1500	1250	1250
Labour usage (£)	42,000	8000	13000	10500	10500
Overheads	2,500	500	1000	500	500

Task 1.3A

TRICKY

The sales data for the last three years have been subject to a time series analysis and the trend is that there is an increase of 2% per quarter in unit sales. The actual unit sales for quarter 4 of last year were 90,000 units. 81081

The time series analysis also shows the following seasonal variations:

Quarter 1   90,000 ÷ 1.11 × 1.02 × .69   −31%

Quarter 2   82708 × 1.02 × .97   −3%

Quarter 3   84357 × 1.02 × 1.23   +23%

Quarter 4   86044 × 1.02 × 1.11   +11%

Forecast the unit sales for each of the four quarters of next year

Quarter 1	57065
Quarter 2	81 826
Quarter 3	105 834
Quarter 4	97419

Task 1.3B

Over the past two years, the sales prices achievable for product X have broadly followed the pattern of inflation in the UK.

What technique might be used when forecasting future sales prices?

Select from:

- Moving averages
- Indexing using the Retail Price Index (RPI) ✗
- Market research
- Linear regression
- Sampling

Task 1.4A

Advertising costs for next year are initially budgeted at £450,000 for 9 equal advertising campaigns. However, a new product will not now be launched which cuts the number of campaigns to 4. Cost saving measures mean that a 5% discount is agreed with the supplier. The advertising budget should be £...190,000....

Select from:

- £450,000
- £190,000
- £210,000
- £210,526
- £50,000

$$\frac{450,000}{9} \times 4 = 200000$$
$$- 5\%$$
$$190,000$$

Task 1.4B

The salaries of the Finance department for the forthcoming year are expected to total £550,680, which includes a 5% annual pay rise.

However, a pay freeze is imposed so the pay rise is not given, but an additional £50,000 bonus is expected for the Finance Director.

The revised budgeted salary costs for the Finance department are ..574,457

Select from:

- £524,457
- £574,457
- £575,680
- £523,146
- £548,146

Task 1.4C

The budgeted labour hours for the forthcoming four-week period are 20,900. There are 140 employees, working a 38 hour week.

In order to increase inventory (stock) to cope with increased demand expected later in the year, more units of product B are to be produced in the coming period than were originally budgeted.

Product B requires 6 minutes of labour time and 0.75 kg of material per unit. 2% of produced units are rejected as faulty.

3,000 extra kg of material can be sourced for the forthcoming month.

Complete the following:

The number of available labour hours in the forthcoming period is..**21,280**..

The number of spare labour hours is..**380**..which would allow ..**3800**.. extra units to be produced.

The extra material could make..**4000**..extra units.

Therefore, the limiting factor is..**LAB HOURS**..so ..**3800**..extra units can be produced.
The number of fault-free units that can be produced is..**3724**..

●●●

Task 1.5

The budgeted output for the quarter was 428,000 units, but 467,800 units were in fact produced.

The total budgeted hours of labour were 642,000. The actual hours worked were 748,500.

The managing director is pleased as he thinks greater output means the workers are being more efficient.

Suggest and explain performance measures or indicators that the managing director could use to investigate the performance of workers.

●●●

Task 1.6

The budget for the next three months is as follows. You are required to complete the cash flow forecast for February

	December	January	February
Production (units)	8,000	10,000	12,000
Sales (units)	8,000	8,000	10,000

(handwritten: 164,000 — 164,000 — 205,000 / 41,000)

The selling price is £20.50 per unit.

The raw material costs £4 per unit.

Wages and other variable costs are £8 per unit.

Other fixed costs are £1,800 per month.

20% of sales are for cash, the remainder being paid in full 60 days following delivery.

Material purchases are paid one month after delivery and are held in inventory (stock) for one month before entering production.

Wages, variable and fixed costs are paid in the month of production.

A new machine costing £450,000 is to be purchased in February to cope with the planned expansion of demand. 20% of payment is to be made on 1 February and the remainder later in the year.

An advertising campaign is also due to be launched, involving a payment of £20,000 in February.

	February
	£
Cash receipts:	
Sales	172,200
Total receipts	
Cash payments:	
Purchases 12,000 × 4 *(PURCHASE JAN FOR FEB. PROD + PAYMENT)*	48,000
Wages and other variable costs	96,000
Fixed costs	1800
Advertising	20 000
Capital expenditure	90 000
Total payments	*(255,800)*
Net cash flow for the month	(83 600)
Opening balance	211,725
Closing balance	128,125

Section 2

Task 2.1

Given below is a summary of the variances for a manufacturing business for the last month. The variances were calculated by comparing the flexed budget to actual results.

Variances – March 20X9

	Variances	
	Adverse	*Favourable*
	£	£
Materials	17,520	
Labour	300	
Fixed overhead expenditure		7,490

A number of factors about the month's production have been discovered:

- at the end of the previous month a new warehouse had been purchased which has meant a saving in warehouse rental

- six new machines were installed at the start of the month which are more power efficient than the old machines, but also more expensive, causing a larger depreciation charge

- there was an unexpected increase in the materials price during the month and when other suppliers were contacted it was found that they were all charging approximately the same price for the materials

- a higher than normal skilled grade of labour was used during the month due to staff shortages. The production process is a skilled process and the benefit has been that these employees, although more expensive, have produced the goods faster and with less wastage. This particular group of employees are also keen to work overtime and, as the business wishes to build up inventory (stock) levels, advantage of this has been taken.

Suggest what effect the combination of the factors given above might have had on the reported variances and make suggestions as to any action that should be taken in light of these factors.

Explain the steps that should be taken when setting budgets, if they are to be successful in motivating staff.

Task 2.2

The budgeted and actual performance for a month is given below.

Flex the budget to the actual activity level, given the information below about costs and show whether each variance is favourable or adverse.

	Budget	Flexed budget	Actual	Variance Fav/(Adv)
	36,000	35,000	35,000	
	£	£	£	£
Revenue (turnover)	1,440,000	1,400,000	1,365,000	(35,000)
Material	432,000	420,000	437,500	(17,500)
Labour	216,000	210,000	203,000	7000
Light, heat, power	92,000	90,000	85,500	4500
Depreciation	100,000	100,000	70,000	30000
Administration	220,000	220,000	230,000	(10,000)
Marketing	180,000	180,000	190,000	(10,000)
Profit	200,000	180,000	149,000	(31,000)

Material and labour costs are variable.

The costs for light, heat and power is semi-variable. The budgeted fixed element is £20,000.

The budget for marketing costs is stepped, increasing every 10,000 units.

Depreciation and administration costs are fixed.

....

PRACTICE ASSESSMENT 1
BUDGETING

ANSWERS

Section 1

Task 1.1A

Installation of anti-virus software on the computer system	IT
Cash collection from customers and clients	Finance
Preparing for the organisation's annual audit	Finance
Advising employees on anti-discrimination laws	HR
Setting up the organisation's private health insurance scheme	HR
Collecting a petty cash float from the bank	Finance
Repairing broken machinery	Maintenance

Task 1.1B

Hire of mini-buses which seat 12 people each	Stepped
Theatre tickets	Variable
Photocopying of permission letters to parents on the school photocopier which is rented.	Semi-variable

Task 1.1C

Client entertaining at horse racing	Marketing department
Repair of security alarm system in offices	Administration department
Sick pay for production manager	Production department
Bonuses for sales managers	Sales team
Depreciation of production equipment	Production department
Cost of recruiting new sales manager	Sales team

Task 1.1D

Redecorating outside of head office building	Revenue
Purchase of new machine	Capital
Replacement of blades on cutting machine	Revenue
Cost of hire-car for managing director to attend meeting in London	Revenue

Practice assessment 1: answers

Task 1.1E

The cost of advertising in a local newspaper	Newspaper's rate card
National insurance rates for the coming year	HM Revenue & Customs
Raw material costs	Prior period invoices
Costs of new equipment/machinery	Sales brochures

Task 1.2A

Hours available: 10 x 30 + 10 x 40 = 700

Units = 700/1.25 = 560

Task 1.2B

Closing inventory (stock) = 80% x 34,500 kg = 27,600 kg

Materials purchases = usage + closing inventory (stock) – opening inventory (stock) = 168,000 + 27,600 – 34,500 = 161,100 kg

Materials purchases cost = £1.20 x 161,000 = £193,320

Task 1.2C

	Month 1	Month 2	Month 3
Sales (units)	12,000	15,000	10,000
Opening inventory (stock) (units)	800	1,300	1,800
Production (balancing figure) (units)	12,500	15,500	10,500
Closing inventory (stock) (units)	1,300	1,800	2,300
Labour cost (£)	31,250	38,750	26,250

You are given the opening inventory (stock) figure, so can calculate the closing and opening inventory (stock) figures for the rest of the three months. From this, with sales, you can calculate the production figures (sales + closing inventory (stock) – opening inventory (stock) = production). (Alternatively, production is always 500 units more than sales in each month). In labour terms, each unit costs ¼ (15 minutes) x £10 per hour = £2.50.

Task 1.2D

Labour hours required = 1,360 x 0.5 = 680 hours

Number of supervisors required = 680/200 = 4 (round up)

Weekly cost = £500 x 4 = £2,000

Task 1.2E

Labour

	Total four weeks	Week 1	Week 2	Week 3	Week 4
Production and sales (units)	10,000	2,000	3,000	2,500	2,500
Material usage (£) (W1)	5,000	1,000	1,500	1,250	1,250
Labour usage (£)	42,000	8,000	13,000	10,500	10,500
Overheads (£)	2,500	500	1,000	500	500

Workings

Material cost per unit = 5,000/10,000 = £0.5 per unit

Labour usage for 2,000 units = 2,000 x 0.5 = 1,000 hours (also the available basis time)

Labour cost for 2,000 units = 1,000 hours x £8 = £8,000

Labour cost for 3,000 units = 1,000 hours x £8 + 500 hours x £10 = £13,000

Labour cost for 2,500 units = 1,000 hours x £8 + 250 hours x £10 = £10,500

Task 1.3A

	Trend	Seasonal variation		Forecast
Quarter 1 (90,000/1.11) x 1.02)	82,703	x 0.69	=	57,065
Quarter 2 (82,703 x 1.02)	84,357	x 0.97	=	81,826
Quarter 3 (84,357 x 1.02)	86,044	x 1.23	=	105,834
Quarter 4 (86,044 x 1.02)	87,765	x 1.11	=	97,419

Practice assessment 1: answers

Task 1.3B

Indexing using the Retail Price Index (RPI)

Task 1.4A

Cost per campaign initially = £450,000/9 = £50,000

Cost of 4 campaigns at a 5% discount = 4 x 95% x 50,000 = £190,000

Task 1.4B

Costs before pay rise = 550,680 x 100/105 = £524,457

Costs plus bonus = £524,457 + £50,000 = £574,457

Task 1.4C

The number of available labour hours in the forthcoming period is 21,280.

The number of spare labour hours is 380 hours which would allow 3,800 extra units to be produced.

The extra material could make 4,000 extra units.

Therefore, the limiting factor is labour so 3,800 extra units can be produced. The number of fault-free units that can be produced is 3,724.

Workings

Number of labour hours available = 140 x 38 x 4 = 21,280

Therefore, spare hours = 21,280 – 20,900 = 380

6 minutes = 0.1 hours

In 380 hours, an extra 380/0.1 = 3,800 units could be produced

3,000 extra kg can be purchased

3,000/0.75 = 4,000 extra units could be produced.

Extra production therefore limited by labour hours, so 3,800 extra units can be produced.

2% of production is faulty, however, so

3,800 x 98% = 3,724 fault-free units could be produced.

Task 1.5

The number of units produced is larger than budgeted, but so too are the hours used to produce them.

The managing director needs to examine whether the greater production is purely due to the increased hours (increased capacity) or whether the workers are actually working more efficiently.

A possible productivity performance measure is units produced per hour compared with budget. The budget was for 428,000/642,000 = 0.67 per hour. The actual performance was 467,800/748,500 = 0.62 per hour. This means that the workers were actually working less efficiently than budgeted.

The managing director could also look at productivity in terms of units produced per employee.

The number of hours is greater than budgeted, suggesting either an increased number of employees or existing workers working overtime. The managing director therefore could also use the number of employees compared with budgeted performance and the number of basic hours, and overtime hours compared with budget.

Further analysis could then look at productivity of new versus existing employees (ie the number produced per employee for each of these two categories), The learning effect may improve the productivity of new employees with time.

Alternatively if overtime was worked, he could compare the number produced per basic labour hour, with the number produced per overtime hour (which may be less if workers are fatigued from long shifts).

Task 1.6

	February
	£
Cash receipts:	
Sales (W1)	172,200
Total receipts	
Cash payments:	
Purchases (W2)	48,000
Wages and other variable costs (W3)	96,000
Fixed costs	1,800
Advertising	20,000
Capital expenditure (W4)	90,000
Total payments	
Net cash flow for the month	(83,600)
Opening balance	211,725
Closing balance	128,125

Workings

1. Sales

    Sales in February = £20.50 x 10,000 = 205,000

    20% cash received in February = 20% x £205,000 = £41,000

    Sales in December = 8,000 x £20.50 = £164,000

    80% cash received in February = 80% x £164,000 = £131,200

    Total = £41,000 + £131,200 = £172,200

2. Purchases

    Materials for February are bought in January but paid for in February, so materials for February = £4 x 12,000 = £48,000

3. Wages and other variable costs, paid for in month incurred so

    12,000 x £8 = £96,000

4. Capital expenditure = 20% x £450,000 = £90,000

Section 2

Task 2.1

New warehouse – this will have the effect of simply reducing the fixed overhead expense (assuming the rent saved exceeds any new depreciation charge) and therefore is part of the favourable fixed overhead expenditure variance. The standard fixed overhead cost should be adjusted to reflect the rental saving.

New machines – the new machines use less power than the old ones therefore reducing the power costs element of the fixed overhead. The additional depreciation charge however will increase the fixed overhead expense. Once the reduction in power costs and increase in depreciation charge are known then the standard fixed overhead should be adjusted.

Price increase – the price increase will be a cause of the adverse materials variance. The price increase appears to be a permanent one as all suppliers have increased their prices so the standard materials cost should be altered.

Skilled labour – the use of the higher skilled labour would be expected to have a favourable effect on the labour variance The additional expense of the skilled labour and the overtime that has been worked will have had an adverse effect on the labour variance, which has cancelled out the effect of the increased labour efficiency to leave a small adverse labour variance. Unless the use of this grade of labour is likely to be a permanent policy then there should be no change to the standard labour rate or hours.

The use of the higher skilled labour would also have a favourable effect on the materials variance due to decreased wastage. However, the adverse effect of the increased price much exceeds this positive effect on materials, leading to the £17,520 adverse variance.

Steps if budgets are to motivate staff

Managers should participate in setting the budgets.

The budgets should be agreed with all parties.

Targets should be challenging but attainable.

All known external (non-controllable) factors should be included in the forecasts.

Managers should be appraised only on costs within their budget and which they can control.

Budgets should be reviewed during the period to which they relate, and revised for factors beyond the control of managers.

Task 2.2

	Budget	Flexed budget	Actual	Variance
	36,000	35,000	35,000	
	£	£	£	£
Revenue (turnover) (W1)	1,440,000	1,400,000	1,365,000	35,000 A
Material (W2)	432,000	420,000	437,500	17,500 A
Labour (W3)	216,000	210,000	203,000	7,000 F
Light, heat, power (W4)	92,000	90,000	85,500	4,500 F
Depreciation	100,000	100,000	70,000	30,000 F
Administration	220,000	220,000	230,000	10,000 A
Marketing (W5)	180,000	180,000	190,000	10,000 A
Profit	200,000	180,000	149,000	31,000 A

Workings

1. Budgeted selling price per unit

   Revenue (turnover)/sales volume

   £1,440,000/36,000 = £40

   Flexed budget: 35,000 x £40 = £1,400,000

2. Budgeted material cost

   £432,000/36,000 = £12

   Flexed budget: 35,000 x £12 = £420,000

3. Budgeted labour cost

   £216,000/36,000 = £6

   Flexed budget: 35,000 x £6 = £210,000

4. Budgeted light, heat, power cost.

   Fixed element = £20,000

   Original budget, variable element = £92,000 − £20,000 = £72,000

   Variable element per unit = £72,000/36,000 = £2 per unit

   Flexed budget 35,000 x £2 = £70,000

   Total flexed cost = £20,000 + £70,000 = £90,000

5. Budgeted marketing cost is stepped, but original and flexed budget in the same range so flexed budget = £180,000.

PRACTICE ASSESSMENT 2
BUDGETING

Time allowed: 2 hours 30 minutes

Section 1

Task 1.1A

An organisation has the following departments:

- Sales team
- Finance department
- Property team
- HR department
- Marketing team

Assign the following purposes to the departments listed:

Purpose

- Prepares the draft financial statements of the organisation FINANCE
- Ensures the business manages its staff correctly, including adhering to employment law   HR
- Promotes the organisation in the market place MARK
- Finds and secures new customers SALES
- Responsible for decisions concerning the buildings from which the organisation trades PROPER
- Prepares the quarterly VAT return/annual tax returns for company and employment taxes   FINANCE

···

Task 1.1B

State whether the following departments or functions should be treated as investment centres, profit centres or cost centres:

- Sales team working on commission and each provided with a company car INV
- Marketing department which organises events to entertain clients COST
- Free canteen for staff in a factory COST

···

Task 1.1C

A factory has two production departments, assembly and finishing. The factory incurs the following overheads:

- Rent and rates FA
- Canteen expenses STAFF
- Inventory (stock) insurance AV . STOCK

From the list below, select the most appropriate method of attributing these overheads between the two departments:

- Number of staff employed
- Floor area
- Units produced
- Average inventory (stock) held

Task 1.1D

Budgets of a manufacturing company:

- Labour
- Material
- Sales and marketing
- Administration
- Capital

State in which of the above budgets the following items of expenditure would be included:

- Legal fees regarding late payment by customers ADMIN
- Advertising costs S & M
- Cost of new computer system for office CAP
- Depreciation costs of new computer system ADMIN
- Cost of annual audit ADMIN
- Wastage costs incurred on production line MAT

Task 1.1E

The following information relates to the cost of material A used in a product.

- £4 per kg – cost of the material at the beginning of the last year
- £6 per kg – cost of the material at the end of the last year
- £6.50 per kg – cost agreed in a contract between the company and its supplier for the coming year.

Which information would you use in the materials budget for the coming year?

£6.50

Task 1.1F

A cost has the following value at different activity levels.

Units	Cost £
10,000	50,000
15,000	65,000
20,000	80,000

What would be the cost at an activity level of 12,000 units?

Select from:

- £60,000
- £48,000
- £36,000
- £52,000
- £56,000

Task 1.2A

Closing inventory (stock) is expected to be 10% more than opening inventory (stock) for each month.

Complete the following

	July	August	September
Opening inventory (stock)	500	550	605
Production	1050	1055	1060
Sales	1,000	1,000	1,000
Closing inventory (stock)	550	605	665

Task 1.2B

50 workers are each expected to work 1,800 hours a year basic time. 10% of this time is idle time. Each unit requires 15 minutes of labour time but 3% of units are rejected as defective. How many non-defective units can be produced?

Select from:

- 360,000
- 384,120
- 19,643
- 314,280
- 24,008

$50 \times 1800 = 90,000$ HRS

$90000 \times -90 = 81,000$ HRS

$81.000 \times 4 = 324,000$ p

$324.000 \times -97 = 314,280$

Task 1.2C

The sales budget is for 200,000 units in the period. The opening inventory (stock) is 18,000 units and closing inventory (stock) is 35,000 units. Each unit requires 3kg of material. The materials usage budget is ....kg

Select from:

- 549,000
- 600,000
- 651,000
- 66,667
- 72,333

```
200000
  35,000
235,000
- 18,000
217.000
  ×3  651,000
```

Task 1.2D

Three products contain a material X as follows:

	Material X kg per unit	Production budget (units)	
A	5	1,000	5000
B	2	2,000	4000
C	1	500	500
			9500

The production process for each product wastes 2% of material.

The materials usage budget in kg is ....9694..

• •

Task 1.3A

A product requires 1 kg of material per unit, 0.5 labour hours per unit and 5 machine minutes per unit. The demand for the product is 10,000 units per month.

Available material is 12,000 kg.   12 000 UNITS

Available labour is 30 workers, each working 180 hours per month. 5400 HRS

Available machines are 2 machines, each working 720 hours per month.

The limiting factor is

A   Sales demand

B   Material

C   Labour hours

D   Machine hours

• •

Task 1.3B

The production budget is limited by labour hours for the coming period of 2,500 hours. This allows for production of 5,000 units.

However, complaints about quality have led to the introduction of a further process in manufacture, which requires an extra 15 minutes per unit.

The revised production budget is ....3333 UNITS.....................

• •

$$\frac{2500}{.5 + .25} = 3333$$

Task 1.3C

The budgeted cost for electricity for the coming month includes an approximately fixed element of £2,000 plus a variable element depending on machine hours. The total budgeted cost for the period, for which 1,000 machine hours are budgeted is £3,500.

However, one machine has to be taken out of service in the coming month to be repaired. This will reduce machine hours to 950 hours. There has also been a sudden increase in electricity charges by 10% to reflect a rise in energy prices.

The revised budgeted electricity cost is ......£3768....................................

Task 1.4

The budget for the next three months is as follows. You are required to complete the cash flow forecast for January, February and March.

The company buys goods, packs them and sells them.

Sales for November and December were £10,000 each month and are forecast to increase by 20% each month from January onwards.

All sales are on credit and receivables (debtors) settle as follows:

▪ 30% in month of sale

▪ 50% in month following sale

▪ 20% in month two months after sale

The company has a gross profit of 40%.

Unpacked units are bought in the month they are sold. The company also has a policy of maintaining a inventory (stock) level at the end of each month equal to 20% (in volume terms) of the following month's sales. Suppliers allow one month's credit.

Fixed overheads of £2,500 are paid in the month incurred.

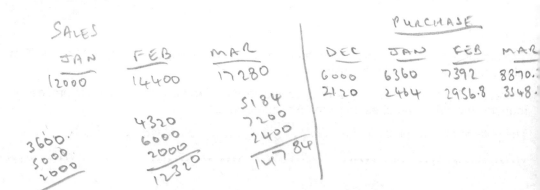

Complete the following cash flow forecast.

	January	February	March
	£	£	£
Cash receipts:			
Sales	10,600	12 320	14784
Total receipts			
Cash payments:			
Purchases			
Fixed overheads	2500	2500	2500
Total payments			
Net cash flow for the month			
Opening balance (overdraft)	(10,000)		
Closing balance			

Task 1.5

An organisation provides training for students wishing to pass professional examinations.

Data collected includes:

- Number of courses
- Number of students
- Number of qualifications awarded

Write a memo to the head of the organisation, recommending four performance indicators that could be used to measure the quality of the organisation's service, against budget. You are not restricted to using only the data listed above.

Task 1.6A

The trend figures for sales in units for a business for the four quarters of last year and the seasonal variations are estimated as:

	Trend unit sales	Seasonal variations
Quarter 1	160,000 units	+7%
Quarter 2	164,500 units	+9%
Quarter 3	169,000 units	−3%
Quarter 4	173,500 units	−13%

Forecast the unit sales for each of the four quarters of next year

Quarter 1	178,000 × 1.07	190.460
Quarter 2	182.500 × 1.09	198.925
Quarter 3	187,000 × 0.97	181.390
Quarter 4	191500 × .87	166 605

Task 1.6B

Complete the table for the budget for January, given the following information :

Material costs are variable.

The company has 25 workers working equal basic hours each month, totalling 2,000 per worker in the year. Labour costs £9 per hour basic time, and £11 per hour overtime. Each unit requires 0.5 hours of labour.

Administrative costs are incurred evenly through the year.

	Budget for the year	Budget for January
Sales units	100,000	8,333
Production units	105,000	9,000
	£	£
Sales	5,000,000	416650
Materials used	472,500	40500
Labour	477,500	41166
Administrative expenditure	24,000	2000

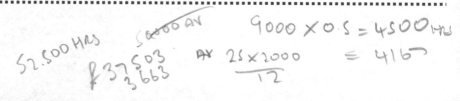

52.500 HRS

£375,03
3,663

5000 AV

AV 25×2000
        12

9000 × 0.5 = 4500 HRS
            = 416?

Section 2

Task 2.1

Details of the budget and actual results for a year in a business are reproduced below.

Operating results					
			Budget		Actual
Volume (units)			20,000		22,000
	£		£	£	£
Revenue (turnover)			960,000		1,012,000
Direct costs					
Materials	240,000			261,800	
Production labour	260,000			240,240	
Light, heat and power	68,000			65,560	
	568,000			567,600	
Fixed overheads	400,000			370,000	
Cost of sales			968,000		937,600
Operating profit/(loss)			(8,000)		74,400

You are given the following information.

■ The budget assumed no closing finished inventory (stock). Actual production was 25,000 units and actual sales 22,000 units.

■ Production employees are paid per week, irrespective of production levels. The employees assumed in the budget are capable of producing up to 26,000 units.

■ The cost of material varies directly with production.

■ The cost of light, heat and power includes a fixed standing charge. In the budget this fixed charge was calculated to be £20,000 per year. However, competition resulted in the supplier reducing the actual charge to £12,000 for the year.

■ During the year, 25,000 units were produced. The 3,000 units of closing finished inventory (stock) were valued on the basis of direct cost plus 'normal' fixed overheads.

■ The number of units was used to apportion direct costs between the cost of sales and closing finished inventory (stock).

■ The budgeted fixed overhead of £20 per unit was used to calculate the fixed overheads in closing finished inventory (stock).

■ The detailed composition of the actual figures for cost of sales and closing inventory (stock) using these policies was as follows.

	Closing finished inventory (stock)	Cost of sales	Cost of production
Units	3,000	22,000	25,000
	£	£	£
Material	35,700	261,800	297,500
Production labour	32,760	240,240	273,000
Light, heat and power	8,940	65,560	74,500
Fixed overheads	60,000	370,000	430,000
	137,400	937,600	1,075,000

You are required to prepare a flexible budget statement, including variances, using a marginal costing approach, as follows. To do this, calculate

The budgeted unit selling price ......48..................

The budgeted material cost per unit .....12..............

The budgeted marginal cost of light, heat and power per unit

...............2.40...

The actual marginal cost of light, heat and power per unit

............55.000 ÷ 22.000 = 2.50.....................

	Flexible budget	Actual results	Variance
Sales units	22,000 units	22,000 units	
	£	£	£
Revenue (turnover)	1.056,000	1,012,000	(44,000)
Variable costs			
Material costs	(264,000)	(261,800)	2200
Variable light, heat and power	(52,800)	(55,000)	(2200)
Contribution	739.200	695,200	(44,000)
Fixed costs			
Production labour	(260,000)	(273,000)	(13,000)
Light, heat and power	(20,000)	(12,000)	8,000
Fixed overheads	(400,000)	(430,000)	(30,000)
Operating profit/(loss)	59.200	(19,800)	(79,000)

Task 2.2

You are required to review the operating statement, and the background information provided and to make recommendations as set out below.

Operating statement

	Flexed budget	Actual	Variance Fav/(Adverse)
	£	£	£
Revenue (turnover)	12,400,000	11,000,000	(1,400,000)
Material	(2,550,000)	(4,012,500)	(1,462,500)
Labour	(5,350,000)	(5,800,000)	(450,000)
Variable production overheads	(1,070,000)	(1,085,000)	(15,000)
Fixed production overheads	(535,000)	(791,250)	(256,250)
Profit/(loss)	2,895,000	(688,750)	(3,583,750)

The business manufactures chocolates.

During the period, the world's largest supplier of the raw material, cocoa, purchased a competitor and was able to push prices upwards given its large market share. The business switched suppliers several times, but this led to quality issues.

During the summer, one of the two machines for production broke down. This led to the machine being out of service for two weeks while a specialist carried out extensive repairs.

Following the decision to stop giving inventory (stock) away free to staff, the workforce slowed their production for three weeks until management reversed their decision.

Write a memo to the Managing Director in which you:

Suggest possible reasons for the variances on materials, labour, fixed production overheads and sales.

Explain actions that should be taken in relation to setting the following year's budget, in the light of these variances.

....

PRACTICE ASSESSMENT 2
BUDGETING

ANSWERS

Section 1

Task 1.1A

Prepares the draft financial statements of the organisation – **Finance department**

Ensures the business manages its staff correctly, including adhering to employment law – **HR department**

Promotes the organisation in the market place – **Marketing team**

Finds and secures new customers – **Sales team**

Responsible for decisions concerning the buildings from which the organisation trades – **Property team**

Prepares the quarterly VAT return/annual tax returns for company and employment taxes – **Finance department**

Task 1.1B

Sales team working on commission and each provided with a company car – Investment centre

Marketing department which organises events to entertain clients – cost centre

Free canteen for staff in a factory – cost centre

Task 1.1C

Rent and rates	Floor area
Canteen expenses	Number of staff employed
Inventory (stock) insurance	Average inventory (stock) held

Task 1.1D

Legal fees regarding late payment by customers	Administration
Advertising costs	Sales and marketing
Cost of new computer system for office	Capital
Depreciation costs of new computer system	Administration
Cost of annual audit	Administration
Wastage costs incurred on production line	Material

Task 1.1E

£6.50 per the contract.

....

Task 1.1F

Answer: £56,000

Working

20,000 units	£80,000
10,000 units	£50,000

£30,000 variable cost for 10,000 units = £3/unit

Therefore, fixed cost = £50,000 – 10,000 x £3 = £20,000

12,000 units cost = £20,000 + £3 x 12,000 = £56,000

....

Task 1.2A

	July	August	September
Opening inventory (stock)	500	550	605
Production	1,050	1,055	1,060
Sales	1,000	1,000	1,000
Closing inventory (stock)	550	605	665

....

Task 1.2B

Hours worked = 50 x 1,800 = 90,000

Productive hours = 90,000 x 90% = 81,000 hours

Hours per unit = 0.25

Units produced = 81,000/0.25 = 324,000

Non-defective units = 97% x 324,000 = 314,280

....

Task 1.2C

Production budget = sales + closing inventory (stock) – opening inventory (stock) = 200,000 + 35,000 – 18,000 = 217,000 units.

Materials usage = 217,000 x 3kg = 651,000 kg

....

Task 1.2D

Material required:

Product A: 5kg x 1,000 = 5,000 kg

Product B: 2kg x 2,000 = 4,000 kg

Product C: 1kg x 500 = 500kg

Total = 9,500kg

Total including wastage = 9,500 x 100/98 = 9,694 kg

••

Task 1.3A

Material required for sales demand = 10,000 x 1kg = 10,000 kg

Available material is 12,000 kg so not a limiting factor.

Labour hours required = 0.5 x 10,000 = 5,000 hours

Available labour = 30 x 180 = 5,400 hours so not a limiting factor.

Machine hours required = 5/60 x 10,000 = 834

Machine hours available = 2 x 720 = 1,440 so not a limiting factor.

Therefore, sales demand is the limiting factor.

••

Task 1.3B

The revised production budget is 3,333 units

Original labour hours per unit = 2,500/5,000 = 0.5 hours per unit

New hours per unit = 0.5 + 0.25 = 0.75

Revised production budget = 2,500/0.75 = 3,333 units

••

Task 1.3C

The revised budgeted electricity cost is £3,768.

Workings:

Electricity = £2,000 plus variable element

Variable = (£3,500 − £2,000)/1,000 = £1.5 per machine hour

Revised cost for 950 hours = £2,000 + (£1.5 x 950) = £3,425

Cost increase = 1.1 x £3,435 = £3,768.

••

Task 1.4

	January £	February £	March £
Cash receipts:			
Sales	10,600	12,320	14,784
Total receipts	**10,600**	**12,320**	**14,784**
Cash payments:			
Purchases	6,240	7,488	8,986
Overheads	2,500	2,500	2,500
Fixed costs	—	—	—
Total payments	**8,740**	**9,988**	**11,486**
Net cash flow for the month	1,860	2,332	3,298
Opening balance (overdraft)	(10,000)	(8,140)	(5,808)
Closing balance	(8,140)	(5,808)	(2,510)

Workings

1. Sales

	Nov £	Dec £	Jan £	Feb £	March £
Sales	10,000	10,000	12,000	14,400	17,280
Receipts					
November	3,000	5,000	2,000		
December		3,000	5,000	2,000	
January			3,600	6,000	2,400
February				4,320	7,200
March					5,184
Total			10,600	12,320	14,784

2. Purchases

	Nov £	Dec £	Jan £	Feb £	March £
Sales	10,000	10,000	12,000	14,400	17,280
Cost of sales		6,000	7,200	8,640	10,368
Opening inventory (stock)		(1,200)	(1,440)	(1,728)	(2,074)
Closing inventory (stock)		1,440	1,728	2,074	2,488
Purchases		6,240	7,488	8,986	10,782
Paid one month later			6,240	7,488	8,986

Task 1.5

To: A Head

From: An Accounting Technician

Date: XX XX XX

Performance Indicators for quality

A number of different indicators can help assess quality. Standards or targets must be set and then the actual performance compared against these.

Many quantitative indicators are given below. However, as the quality of service will also be judged by the students i.e. the customers, I recommend surveys are undertaken at the end of each course to obtain feedback about the quality of service from the students.

Non-financial quantitative indicators:

Percentage of students awarded a qualification

Number of individual exam passes

Number of first time passes per number of exams taken

Pass rates per course

Number of complaints from students

Average marks obtained compared with average for that exam nationwide

Tutorial note: only four indicators are required

Practice assessment 2: answers

Task 1.6A

	Trend x seasonal variation	Forecast
Quarter 1 (+4,500)	178,000 x 1.07	190,460
Quarter 2 (+4,500)	182,500 x 1.09	198,925
Quarter 3 (+4,500)	187,000 x 0.97	181,390
Quarter 4 (+4,500)	191,500 x 0.87	166,605

Task 1.6B

	Budget for the year	Budget for January
Sales units	100,000	8,333
Production units	105,000	9,000
	£	£
Sales	5,000,000	416,650
Materials used	472,500	40,500
Labour	477,500	41,166
Administrative expenditure	24,000	2,000

Workings

1. Sales price per unit = £5,000,000/100,000 = £50
   January sales = 8,333 x £50 = £416,650

2. Material
   Price per unit = £472,500/105,000 = £4.5 per unit
   January materials usage = £4.5 x 9,000 = £40,500

3. Labour
   Labour hours for January = 9,000 x 0.5 = 4,500
   Labour hours available = 2,000 x 25/12 = 4,167
   Labour cost = 4,167 x £9 + (4,500 – 4,167) x £11 = £41,166

232

Section 2

Task 2.1

(1) Budgeted selling price = £960,000 revenue (turnover) ÷ 20,000 units = £48 per unit

(2) Budgeted material cost = £240,000 material cost ÷ 20,000 units

$$= £12 \text{ per unit}$$

(3) Total budgeted marginal cost of light, heat and power

$$= £68,000 - \text{fixed cost } £20,000 = £48,000$$

Budgeted marginal cost of light, heat and power per unit

$$= £48,000 ÷ 20,000 = £2.40 \text{ per unit}$$

(4) Actual marginal cost of light, heat and power

$$= £74,500 \text{ production cost} - \text{fixed costs } £12,000$$

$$= £62,500$$

Actual marginal cost of light, heat and power per unit

$$= £62,500 ÷ 25,000 \text{ units produced} = £2.50 \text{ per unit}$$

Alternatively, from the actual variable costs included in the statement given,

marginal cost = £55,000/22,000 units = £2.50

Flexible budget statement

Sales units	Flexible budget 22,000 units		Actual results 22,000 units		Variance
	£	£	£	£	£
Revenue (turnover)'					
(22,000 × £48 (from (1)))		1,056,000		1,012,000	44,000 (A)
Variable costs					
Material (22,000 × £12)	264,000		261,800		2,200 (F)
Light, heat and power					
(22,000 × £2.40)	52,800		55,000*		2,200 (A)
		316,800		316,800	
Contribution		739,200		695,200	
Fixed costs					
Production labour	260,000		273,000		13,000 (A)
Light, heat and power	20,000		12,000		8,000 (F)
Fixed overheads	400,000		430,000		30,000 (A)
		680,000		715,000	
Operating profit/(loss)		59,200		(19,800)	79,000 (A)

Note: (A) denotes an adverse variance; (F) denotes a favourable variance.

*Variable cost of light, heat and power = £2.50 (from (4)) x 22,000 = £55,000

Task 2.2

To: Managing Director

From: An Accounting Technician

Date: XX XX XX

Reason for variances

Sales variance

As the budget has been flexed, prices were lower than expected per unit. This may have reflected discounting if the brand image had suffered due to quality issues.

Materials variance

There is an adverse materials variance due to the increase in prices by the key supplier. Our attempt to source cocoa from alternative suppliers led to quality problems and so we used more cocoa than expected (adverse usage variance in addition to adverse price variance).

Labour variance

This was partly due to the machine breakdown, when staff were unable to work, but also due to the staff unrest because of the stoppage of free chocolate to staff. Staff were therefore both paid for work when they were idle, and were less efficient because they were less motivated.

Fixed production overheads

The use of specialist engineers to fix the machinery will have contributed to the adverse fixed overheads variance.

Actions

If we cannot source a reliable, cheaper supplier of cocoa then the standard cost of material should be increased in the next budget, to reflect the prices charged by the key supplier.

No amendment should be made to the standards used in the budget in relation to labour, as both occurrences (staff go-slow and machine breakdown) are hopefully not to be repeated.

If not, for example if the breakdown is indicative of the machinery becoming less reliable, it may be necessary to budget for higher maintenance costs within fixed production overheads in future.

If we have had to reduce prices permanently because of image problems, we should amend the standard selling price in the next budget.

PRACTICE ASSESSMENT 3
BUDGETING

Time allowed: 2 hours 30 minutes

Section 1

Task 1.1A

Calculate the appropriate budgeted overhead recovery rate for the following production department. The department's annual budget for indirect costs is:

	£
Supervisor wages	25,000
Rent of factory space	40,000
Depreciation of machinery	15,000
Machine maintenance	8,000
Canteen costs	2,000
Total	90,000

The budgeted production of 9,000 units will require 30,000 machine hours and 6,000 direct labour hours.

Complete the following:

Overhead recovery should be based on labour hours/machine hours/units produced.

The recovery rate will be £....3........ per ..MACHINE HOUR

· ·

Task 1.1B

Select the appropriate budget for the following items of expenditure:

Expenditure	Budget
Annual service cost of equipment	REPAIRS & MAINT
Depreciation of printer used to produce marketing brochures	MARK
Fuel costs for delivery trucks	DIST.
Purchase of new delivery truck	CAP
Depreciation of delivery truck	DIST

Select from:

- Distribution budget
- Marketing budget
- Repairs and maintenance budget
- Capital budget

Task 1.1C

Select an appropriate accounting treatment for each of the following costs:

Expenditure	Accounting treatment
Material wastage	DIRECT
Companies House penalty for late filing	ADMIN O/H
Food and drink at opening of new showroom	MARK O/H
Cost of purchasing manager	ACTIVITY PRODUCT COST
Room hire for office staff training course	ADMIN O/H
Material storage costs	ACTIVITY PRODUCTED GST
Machinery maintenance costs	PROD M/C HOUR O/H

Select from:

- Activity-based charge to production cost centres
- Allocate to marketing overheads
- Allocate to administrative overheads
- Charge to production at a machine hour overhead rate
- Direct cost

Task 1.1D

Select an appropriate source which will provide, or help you forecast, the following information when constructing a budget.

Information required	Source
Foreign exchange rates	FT
National Insurance Contribution rates	HM REVENUE
Interest rates on factory mortgage	LOAN AGREEMENT
Sales demand of a new product	MARKET RESEARCH
Irrecoverable (bad) debts	CREDIT CONTROL
Directors' bonuses	BOARD MINS.

Select from:

- Market research consultant
- HM Revenue & Customs website
- Credit controller
- Loan agreement
- Articles of Association of Company
- Board minutes
- The Financial Times

Task 1.2A

Complete the following production budget for a product.

Closing inventory (stock) is to be 20% of the next period's sales. Sales in period 4 will be 12,000 units.

Units of product

	Period 1	Period 2	Period 3
Opening inventory (stock)	2,200	2300	2340
Production	11,100	11540	11760
Sales	11,000	11,500	11,700
Closing inventory (stock)	2300	2340	2400

Task 1.2B

The next three months' production budget is shown below. Of the completed units, 2% fail a quality test and are scrapped.

How many units must be manufactured to allow for the scrapped units?

	Month 1	Month 2	Month 3
Required units	18,000	20,000	15,000
Manufactured units	18368	20.409	15307

Task 1.2C

A product uses a material P in its production. P costs £3 per litre. The materials purchasing budget for material P in the next quarter is being constructed. The budgeted production is 5,000 units in the next quarter.

Each unit of product uses 0.75 litres of P, but a further 0.05 litres is lost in wastage for every unit made. There will be inventory (stock) levels of 345 litres of P at the start of the quarter, but inventory (stock) of only 150 litres is required at the end of the quarter. The materials purchasing budget (in £) for the coming next quarter is

Select from:

- £3,805
- £4,195
- £11,415
- £12,585

$.75 + 0.05 = 0.8$ LTRS
$\times 5000$
4000 LTRS.
$+ 150$
4150
$- 345$
3805 LTRS.

$\dfrac{3805}{3}$
11415

Task 1.2D

A company makes two products, A and B, using the same grade of labour. The company pays 10 employees for a 35 hour week, regardless of whether all hours are worked, at a rate of £10 per hour. Overtime is paid at £12 per hour.

Product A requires 0.5 labour hours

Product B requires 2 labour hours

The budgeted production for the next four week period is

Product A   500 units $\times 0.5 = 250$ HRS

Product B   500 units $\times 2 = 1000$ HRS

No O/TIME

350
4
1400 HRS.
$\times 10$
£14,000

240

What is the labour cost budget for the next four week period?

Select from:

- £12,500
- £12,600
- (£14,000)
- £16,100

....

Task 1.2E

A company has a production budget for the coming month of 16,800 units.

Details of the production overheads are:

Factory rental – this is £180,000 per annum.

Purchasing department – previous periods have shown that at a production level of 12,000 units per month the purchasing department costs totalled £76,000, and at a production level of 18,000, the costs totalled £94,000.

Supervisor costs – a supervisor is required for every 5,000 units made. The cost of one supervisor is £15,000.

Complete the overhead budget for the coming month:

	£
Factory rental	15,000
Purchasing department	90,400
Supervisor costs	60,000
Total	165,400

....

241

Task 1.2F

You are required to complete the following working schedules and operating budget for production of 16,000 units. 1000

Working schedules

Materials

	Kg	£
Opening inventory (stock)	500	1,000
Purchases	2,400	6,000
Sub-total	2,900	7,000
Usage	2450	5875
Closing inventory (stock)	450	1125

Closing inventory (stock) of raw material is to be valued at budgeted purchase price

Labour

	Hours	£
Basic time @ £15 per hour	1400	21000
Overtime	200	4500
Total	1600	25,500

Each unit takes 6 minutes. There are 1,400 basic labour hours available. Overtime is paid at time and a half

Overhead

	Hours	£
Variable @ £0.80 per hour	1600	1280
Fixed		4,000
Total		5280

Variable overhead recovered on total labour hours

Operating budget

	Units	£
Sales @ £2.40 each	15,000	36.000
Opening inventory (stock)	-	
Cost of production	16,000	
Materials		5875
Labour		25500
Overhead		5280
Total production cost		36655
Closing inventory (stock) of finished goods	1,000	– 2291
Cost of goods sold		34364
Gross profit		1636

Closing inventory (stock) of finished goods is valued at budgeted production cost per unit.

••

Task 1.3A

Last year sales were £4,000,000.

Analysis of recent years shows a growth trend of 8% per annum.

The seasonal variation has been:

Quarter	£
Quarter 1	−£10,000
Quarter 2	+£25,000
Quarter 3	+£35,000
Quarter 4	−£50,000

Forecast the income for each quarter of the coming year.

Quarter	£
Quarter 1	1,070,000
Quarter 2	1,105,000
Quarter 3	1,115,000
Quarter 4	1,030,000
Year	4,320,000

....

Task 1.3B

The direct materials cost for quarters 2 and 3 are estimated in terms of quarter 1 prices as £235,800 and £219,300 respectively. The quarter 1 price index for materials is 218.0 and the price indices are estimated at 235.2 and 240.8 for quarters 2 and 3 respectively.

Complete the following:

	Quarter 2	Quarter 3
Forecast direct material costs £	254404	242236

....

Task 1.3C

A company is launching a new product into the market place.

What technique would be most useful when forecasting the product's future sales price?

Select from:

- Moving averages
- Indexing using the Retail Price Index (RPI)
- Market research
- Linear regression
- Hi-lo

....

Task 1.4

The following budget has been constructed for a year.

	Budget for the year	Budget for month 1
Sales forecast (units)	200,000	16,000
Production budget (units)	180,000	14,000
	£	£
Sales	900,000	72,000
Materials used	270,000	21,000
Labour	36,000	2800
Variable production overhead	180,000	14000
Variable selling overhead	100,000	8000
Fixed overheads	58,000	4833

Material, labour and variable production overheads are variable with the number of units produced.

Variable selling overheads vary with units sold.

Fixed overheads are incurred evenly throughout the year.

Complete the budget for month 1.

....

Task 1.5

You have been responsible for preparing a cash budget. An extract is given below showing cash inflows.

Cash budget

	This year's actual cash inflows £	Next year £
Cash inflows from sales	185,000	179,000
Proceeds from sale of car		14,000

You have constructed the budget with reference to this year's cash inflows and the following information.

Sales are expected to remain constant. Receivables (debtors) at the end of this year are £30,000. Historically, year end receivables are kept at this level but they are expected to increase by 20% by the end of next year.

The managing director's car is sold every two years at a loss of around £10,000, and replaced with a better model.

The managing director is concerned that sales appear to be decreasing in this cash budget, and asks for an explanation regarding the car sale.

Write an email to the Managing Director explaining the calculations and assumptions in your cash budget. Address his concern regarding sales and the car transaction.

••

Task 1.6A

The sales team predict that next year total sales will be £4,560,000. This assumes a 5% increase in sales price per unit, and a further 7% increase in sales volume.

However, the production manager says that as the factory is at full capacity, the company will not be able to produce any extra units. Therefore, there will be no increase in sales volume.

The sales forecast should be revised to £ [........................]

Select from:

- £4,332,000

- £4,240,800

$$\frac{4,560,000}{1.07} = 4,261,882$$

- £4,342,857

- £4,261,682

••

Task 1.6B

Next year, insurance premiums are forecast at £345,000. This assumes a 5% increase due to market conditions, and a 10% reduction due to the company seeking a lower level of cover.

The finance director decides that it is too risky to reduce the level of cover, and so the insurance taken out will give the same level of cover as last year.

The insurance premiums forecast should be revised to £ [........................]

Select from:

- £362,250

- £313,636

$$\frac{345,000}{1.05} = \frac{328,571.42}{90} \times 100$$

- £328,571

$$= 365,079.35 \times 1.05$$

- £383,333

••

Task 1.6C

A company has budgeted to make and sell 50,000 units in the next 7 day period.

The information regarding the production of units is as follows:

One unit requires 0.1 labour hours and 0.5 kg of material.

20,000 kg of material have been ordered from the usual supplier at an agreed price. If further supplies are needed, the price will be higher due to the late order.

80 workers work 8 hour days, 7 days a week.

The packaging team can pack 6,000 units a day.

Complete the following analysis:

There is labour available to make ~~44,800~~ units in normal time. Therefore, ~~520~~ hours of overtime will be needed.

The existing raw material order will provide enough material to make ~~40,000~~ units. Therefore ~~5000~~ kg will have to be purchased on the open market.

The packaging team can test ~~42000~~ units in the period. It will be necessary to make alternative arrangements for ~~8000~~ units.

....

Section 2

Task 2.1

You are asked to review the operating statement shown below, and the background information provided, and to make recommendations.

Operating statement for the year ended 30 June 20X6

	Budget £	Actual £	Variance Fav/(adv)
Revenue (turnover)	3,450,000	3,260,000	(190,000)
Variable costs			
Material	1,090,000	1,092,000	(2,000)
Labour	540,000	590,000	(50,000)
Fixed costs			
Marketing & PR	450,000	250,000	200,000
Depreciation	150,000	149,000	1,000
Administration	260,000	254,000	6,000
	960,000	925,000	(35,000)

The budget has been flexed to reflect the actual number of units produced and sold in the year. The original budget had been prepared at the start of the year and no further revisions had been made.

The sales and marketing director was dismissed during the year, as he was found to have been using company marketing funds for personal entertaining. No replacement has yet been found for the director.

The departure of the sale and marketing director led to the cancellation of a large advertising campaign that he had planned for the coming year. The managing director temporarily oversaw the marketing team and decided that a reduction in sales price would be just as effective as a large marketing campaign.

Due to cash flow problems during the year, the company lost a prompt payment discount for one of its main materials. A new bonus initiative for production workers was introduced to discourage materials wastage.

The Managing Director is confused about what the variances mean in terms of the eventful year that the company has had.

Write an email to the Managing Director suggesting possible reasons for the major variances, and advising on any action that should be taken with respect to the standards used when setting the budget for the next year.

Task 2.2

The budgeted and actual performance for a month is given below.

Flex the budget to the actual activity level, given the information below about costs, and show whether each variance is favourable or adverse.

	Budget	Flexed budget	Actual	Variance Fav/(Adv)
Sales volume	100,000	120,000	120,000	
	£	£	£	£
Revenue (turnover)	4,500,000	5,400,000	4,865,000	(535,000)
Material	2,200,000	2,640,000	2,437,500	202,500
Labour	500,000	600,000	518,000	82,000
Light, heat, power	72,000	82,000	90,000	(8,000)
Depreciation	100,000	100,000	90,000	10,000
Administration	220,000	220,000	230,000	(10,000)
Marketing	180,000	180,000	190,000	(10,000)
Profit	1,228,000	1,578,000	1,309,500	(268,500)

Material and labour costs are variable.

The cost for light, heat and power is semi-variable. The budgeted fixed element is £22,000.

The budget for marketing costs is stepped, increasing every 80,000 units.

Depreciation and administration costs are fixed.

22,000

PRACTICE ASSESSMENT 3
BUDGETING

ANSWERS

Section 1

Task 1.1A

Overhead recovery should be based on **machine hours**.

The recovery rate will be **£3** per machine hour.

Working

Overhead recovery = £90,000/30,000 = £3 per machine hour.

Task 1.1B

Expenditure	Budget
Annual service cost of equipment	Repairs and maintenance budget
Depreciation of printer used to produce marketing brochures	Marketing budget
Fuel costs for delivery trucks	Distribution budget
Purchase of new delivery truck	Capital budget
Depreciation of delivery truck	Distribution budget

Task 1.1C

Expenditure	Accounting treatment
Material wastage	Direct cost
Companies House penalty for late filing	Allocate to administrative overheads
Food and drink at opening of new showroom	Allocate to marketing overheads
Cost of purchasing manager	Activity-based charge to production cost centres
Room hire for office staff training course	Allocate to administrative overheads
Material storage costs	Activity-based charge to production cost centres
Machinery maintenance costs	Charge to production at a machine hour overhead rate. (Or - Activity-based charge to production cost centres)

Task 1.1D

Information required	Source
Foreign exchange rates	Financial Times
National Insurance Contribution rates	HM Revenue & Customs website
Interest rates on factory mortgage	Loan agreement
Sales demand of a new product	Market research consultant
Irrecoverable (bad) debts	Credit controller
Directors' bonuses	Board minutes

Task 1.2A

	Period 1	Period 2	Period 3
Opening inventory (stock)	2,200	2,300	2,340
Production	11,100	11,540	11,760
Sales	11,000	11,500	11,700
Closing inventory (stock)	2,300	2,340	2,400

Workings

Closing inventory (stock):

20% x 11,500 = 2,300

20% x 11,700 = 2,340

20% x 12,000 = 2,400

Production = sales + closing inventory (stock) – opening inventory (stock)

Period 1 production = 11,000 + 2,300 – 2,200 = 11,100

Period 2 production = 11,500 + 2,340 – 2,300 = 11,540

Period 3 production = 11,700 + 2,400 – 2,340 = 11,760

Task 1.2B

	Month 1	Month 2	Month 3
Required units	18,000	20,000	15,000
Manufactured units	18,368	20,409	15,307

Workings

18,000 x 100/98 = 18,368 etc – must be rounded up to ensure sufficient units are made after 2% are scrapped.

Task 1.2C

Answer = £**11,415**

Material usage = budgeted production x budgeted usage per unit (including wastage)

= 5,000 x (0.75 + 0.05)

= 4,000 litres

Materials purchases (litres) = closing inventory (stock) + usage – opening inventory (stock)

= 150 + 4,000 – 345

= 3,805 litres

Materials purchase (in £) = £3 x 3,805 = £11,415

Task 1.2D

Answer = £**14,000**

Labour hours required for budgeted production:

Product A 500 x 0.5 = 250 hours

Product B 500 x 2 = 1,000 hours

Total hours required = 250 + 1,000 = 1,250 hours.

Hours available without overtime = 10 x 35 x 4 = 1,400 hours

Therefore no overtime is required, but the company must pay for 1,400 hours at £10 per hour = £14,000

Task 1.2E

	£
Factory rental	15,000
Purchasing department	90,400
Supervisor costs	80,000
Total	185,400

Workings:

Factory rental = £180,000 pa = £180,000/12 = £15,000 per month

Purchasing department costs are semi-variable:

An additional (18,000 – 12,000) = 6,000 units has an additional cost of (£94,000 - £76,000) = £18,000. Variable cost per unit = £18,000/6,000 = £3 per unit.

Therefore, at activity level of 12,000 units:

£76,000 = (£3 x 12,000) + fixed element

So the fixed element = £40,000

Therefore, for 16,800 units, purchasing department costs = £40,000 + (£3 x 16,800) = £90,400

Supervisor costs are stepped. At production of 16,800 units, 16,800/5,000 = 3.36 supervisors are needed. This must be rounded up to 4, so the fixed cost = 4 x £20,000 = £80,000.

4 x 15,000 = 60,000

Task 1.2F

Working schedules

Materials

	Kg	£
Opening inventory (stock)	500	1,000
Purchases	2,400	6,000
Sub-total	2,900	7,000
Usage	2,450	5,875
Closing inventory (stock) (450 x £6,000/2,400)	450	1,125

Labour

	Hours	£
Basic time @ £15 per hour	1,400	21,000
Overtime	200	4,500
Total	1,600	25,500

Overhead

	Hours	£
Variable @ £0.80 per hour	1,600	1,280
Fixed		4,000
Total		5,280

Operating budget

	Units	£
Sales @ £2.40 each	15,000	36,000
Opening inventory (stock)	0	0
Cost of production	16,000	
Materials		5,875
Labour		25,500
Overhead		5,280
Total production cost		36,655
Closing inventory (stock) of finished goods	1,000	2,291
Cost of goods sold		34,364
Gross profit		1,636

Workings

Materials:

Usage = opening inventory (stock) + purchases – closing inventory (stock) = 2,450 kg

Cost of closing inventory (stock) = £6,000/2,400 x 450 = £1,125

Usage price is the balance of £7,000 - £1,125 = £5,875

Labour

Time for production = 16,000 x 6/60 = 1,600 hours, therefore 200 overtime hours are required.

1,400 @ £15 per hour = £21,000

200 @ £15 x 1.5 = £4,500

Overheads = £0.80 x 1,600 = £1,280

Closing inventory (stock) = total production cost/16,000 x 1,000 = £2,291

Deduct from total production cost to give cost of sales £36,655 - £2,291 = £34,364

Task 1.3A

Quarter	£
Quarter 1 (£1,080,000 - £10,000)	1,070,000
Quarter 2 (£1,080,000 + £25,000)	1,105,000
Quarter 3 (£1,080,000 + £35,000)	1,115,000
Quarter 4 (£1,080,000 – £50,000)	1,030,000
Year	4,320,000

Workings

Last year sales = £4,000,000

But trend is 8% growth = 1.08 x £4,000,000 = £4,320,000

Sales per quarter (trend) = £4,320,000/4 = £1,080,000

Task 1.3B

	Quarter 2	Quarter 3
Forecast direct material costs £	254,404	242,236

Workings

Quarter 2

£235,800 x 235.2/218.0 = £254,404

Quarter 3

£219,300 x 240.8/218.0 = £242,236

Task 1.3C

Answer: Market research

Task 1.4

	Budget for the year	Budget for month 1
Sales forecast (units)	200,000	16,000
Production budget (units)	180,000	14,000
	£	£
Sales	900,000	72,000
Materials used	270,000	21,000
Labour	36,000	2,800
Variable production overhead	180,000	14,000
Variable selling overhead	100,000	8,000
Fixed overheads	58,000	4,833

Workings

1. Sales

    Sales price per unit = £900,000/200,000 = £4.50 per unit.

    Therefore, sales of 16,000 units = £4.50 x 16,000 = £72,000

2. Materials

    Materials cost per unit produced (using annual budget) = £270,000/180,000 = £1.50 per unit.

    Material cost of 14,000 units in month 1 = 14,000 x £1.50 = £21,000

3. Labour

    Labour cost per unit produced (from annual budget) = £36,000/180,000 = £0.20

    Labour cost of 14,000 units in month 1 = 14,000 x £0.20 = £2,800

4. Variable production overhead

    Variable production overhead per unit (from annual budget) = £180,000/180,000 = £1.00 per unit

    Variable production overhead costs for month 1 = 14,000 x £1.00 = £14,000

5. Variable selling overheads

    Variable selling overheads per unit (from annual budget) = £100,000/200,000 = £0.50 per unit

    Variable selling overheads for month 1 = 16,000 x £0.50 = £8,000

6. Fixed overheads

    For month 1, fixed overhead = 58,000/12 = £4,833

Task 1.5

To: Managing Director

From: An Accountant

Date; XX XX XX

Subject: Cash budget – inflows

Budget preparation

Sales

I have prepared the cash budget by considering the change in receivable (debtor) balances at the start and end of next year. Receivables are expected to increase by 20%, ie (£30,000 x 1.2) to £36,000. Sales are not decreasing but are expected to be the same as last year. However, as receivables will increase by £6,000 we will collect £6,000 less cash than the sales we actually make.

Last year, there was no change in the receivables balance at the start and end of the year, so the cash collected from sales was therefore equal to those sales (£185,000).

Assuming the same level of sales, and the £6,000 increase in receivables, means we will collect £185,000 - £6,000 = £179,000.

Car

We buy and sell a car for you every two years. The current carrying amount (net book value) of the car in the accounts is £24,000, but it is assumed that we will sell this for a £10,000 loss as in previous years, so the actual proceeds received will be £14,000 as shown in the cash budget.

The extract you have is of the cash inflows only. You need to look at the full cash budget which will show the outflow of cash for the new car being purchased.

• •

Task 1.6A

The sales forecast should be revised to £ **4,261,682**

Workings

Last year's sales x 1.05 x 1.07 = £4,560,000

If the 7% increase in sales volume does not happen:

Sales forecast = last year's sales x 1.05 = £4,560,000/1.07 = £4,261,682

• •

Task 1.6B

The insurance premiums forecast should be revised to **£383,333**.

Workings

Last year's premiums x 1.05 x 90% = £345,000

Without the reduction due to reduced cover:

Forecast = last year's premiums x 1.05 = £345,000/0.90 = £383,333

Task 1.6C

There is labour available to make **44,800** units in normal time. Therefore, **520** hours of overtime will be needed.

The existing raw material order will provide enough material to make **40,000** units. Therefore **5,000** kg will have to be purchased on the open market.

The packaging team can test **42,000** units in the period. It will be necessary to make alternative arrangements for **8,000** units.

Workings

Labour

Time available = 80 x 8 x 7 = 4,480 hours which makes (4,480/0.1) = 44,800 units

Time required = 0.1 x 50,000 = 5,000 hours

Therefore overtime = 5,000 – 4,480 = 520 hours

Material

20,000/0.5 = 40,000 units can be made with the existing order

10,000 x 0.5 = 5,000 kg must be additionally sourced

Packing team can pack 6,000 x 7 = 42,000 units, leaving 8,000 to be packed elsewhere.

Section 2

Task 2.1

To: Managing Director

From: An Accountant

Date: XX XX XX

Subject: Variances for the year ended 30 June 20X6

I explain the variances experienced. They have been calculated using a flexed budget meaning that none of the variances are due to differences in the actual volumes sold or produced compared to the budget.

Revenue (turnover)

The adverse variance is due to the reduction in sales price. It is not due to a change in volume for the reasons stated above. This suggests a 5.5% drop in sales price. If the selling price will continue at this reduced level, this should be adjusted for when preparing the next budget.

Materials

There is only a very small variance in respect of materials costs. However, action has been taken in respect of materials during the year, which suggests that there may be two conflicting factors here.

The loss of the prompt payment discount would mean that the price of materials was more than expected. This would lead to an adverse variance. However the bonus scheme introduced to discourage materials wastage appears to have had a positive effect in reducing materials usage, so counteracting the effect of the increased price.

The materials standard cost should be amended if the bonus scheme is having such an effect and is likely to continue next year. If the cash flow problems were a one-off, then the materials price should not be adjusted in the standard ie it is assumed that the prompt payment discount will be available in future.

Labour

The bonus scheme will have increased the cost of labour, and may be the reason for the adverse labour variance. However, the efficiency of workers should also be considered to see if there has also been an adverse change here. Alternatively, the bonus scheme may be increasing efficiency, in which case the cost of it is causing a very large variance. The cost of the bonus scheme must be weighed up against reduced materials usage and any increased labour efficiency.

Marketing and PR

There is a favourable variance here due to the cancellation of the advertising campaign and also because no sales director's salary has been paid for part of the year. The stoppage of personal expenditure by the former director will have also reduced the marketing costs.

There is no major variance in depreciation or administration.

Task 2.2

	Budget	Flexed budget	Actual	Variance
	100,000	120,000	120,000	
	£	£	£	£
Revenue (turnover) (W1)	4,500,000	5,400,000	4,865,000	535,000A
Material (W2)	2,200,000	2,640,000	2,437,500	202,500F
Labour (W3)	500,000	600,000	518,000	82,000F
Light, heat, power (W4)	72,000	82,000	90,000	8,000A
Depreciation	100,000	100,000	90,000	10,000F
Administration	220,000	220,000	230,000	10,000A
Marketing (W5)	180,000	180,000	190,000	10,000A
Profit	1,228,000	1,578,000	1,309,500	268,500A

Workings

1. Budgeted selling price per unit

   Revenue/sales volume

   £4,500,000/100,000 = £45

   Flexed budget: 120,000 x £45 = £5,400,000

2. Budgeted material cost

   £2,200,000/100,000 = £22

   Flexed budget: 120,000 x £22 = £2,640,000

3. Budgeted labour cost

   £500,000/100,000 = £5

   Flexed budget: 120,000 x £5 = £600,000

4. Budgeted light, heat, power cost

   Fixed element = £22,000

   Original budget, variable element = £72,000 − £22,000 = £50,000

   Variable element per unit = £50,000/100,000 = £0.5 per unit

   Flexed budget variable element 120,000 x £0.5 = £60,000

   Total flexed cost = £22,000 + £60,000 = £82,000

5. Budgeted marketing cost is stepped, but original and flexed budget in the same range so flexed budget = £180,000.

Notes